GROUND WORK

Get Better at Making Better Products

VIDYA DINAMANI & HEATHER SAMARIN

PRAISE FOR GROUNDWORK

Groundwork *is a must read. Dinamani and Samarin do an excellent job of outlining in very practical and easy-to-read stories what are the foundational elements of building any product with clarity and purpose ... and why they are critical to the success of any company!*

Ginny Lee ▪ President and COO at Khan Academy

As a product leader, your job is to build products that delight customers. To do this, you need efficient decision-making, a committed team, and a healthy dose of customer obsession. Groundwork *provides the framework you need to consistently delight customers in ways that energize teams and build a great business.*

Gibson Biddle ▪ former VP/CPO at Netflix/Chegg, now a teacher, speaker, and workshop host

Vidya and Heather bring their tremendous experience leading and teaching the world's best product builders to the page in this roll-up-your sleeves guide. Recommended for product executives who are dedicated to helping their teams make better products.

Brent Tworetzky ▪ Chief Operating Officer at Parsley Health, and Organizer of the New York Product Conference

My son plays football and while everyone wants to work on the "read option" or the "wildcat" or all these fancy concepts, 90% of the game is about blocking and tackling. The simple or basic stuff... and consistent execution of those things... do more to define success than any of the fancy concepts that people spend so much time thinking about. In other words, I think the concept of your book is fantastic. In many ways it's an explanation of why we (our industry) are so far into our journey of building software and we still pump out more failures and mediocre results than winners. You should be really proud of this. It's a great piece of work.

Bill Lucchini ▪ CEO at Dealer-FX Group, Inc

Over the years, I've collaborated directly with Vidya and Heather on difficult product challenges at my company. Let me tell you, they know their stuff! This book helps product teams and executives create lifelong customers by delivering a successful product to the market. My product team is better because we took the best practices found in this book and applied them to our business. Two thumbs up!

Steven Cox ▪ Founder and CEO at TakeLessons.com

Heather and Vidya's incredible success at Intuit and as product management consultants to dozens of companies globally shines through in Groundwork. *The insights here will help your teams create the strong foundation that your products need to not only delight customers, but to generate the results that you expect. The best part is that the guidance is actionable and practical too.*

Morgan Hays ▪ Former VP Product Management and Marketing at TiVo

As a product leader in a complex industry, it's challenging to find great product talent with industry experience. I leverage the techniques learnt from Groundwork *as my guide for ensuring the smart people I hire address the problems they uncover in the best way. It has saved me so much time and effort to ensure they get it right!*

Julie Frahms ▪ Director Consumer Digital Products at Sharp HealthCare

There are many product management methodologies out there. Vidya and Heather have distilled the many concepts into an easily digestible and actionable framework. From the individual product manager looking to improve to the product leader looking for a consistent framework—the problem statement and persona lead the way.

Mykola Konrad ▪ VP Product Management at Brightcove

Groundwork is like a loving parent that doesn't just tell you to eat your damn vegetables, it tells you which vegetables to eat, and how to start enjoying them, so your products have a shot at growing up big and strong. In an age where many product leaders myopically focus on growth hacking their way into rocket-powered unicorn status (which typically fizzles as quickly as it launches), Groundwork calmly and clearly lays out the hard, foundational work upon which are built robust, sustainable, and beloved products that thrive, whether the market is up or down.

Jason Amunwa ▪ Product Management and Growth Expert

Having worked closely with Heather and Vidya, I am excited to see them bring the true craft of great product leadership to others. Their obsession with falling in love with the customer problem truly differentiates them from others. A must-read for product leaders.

Rick Jensen ▪ Chief People & Places Officer at Headspace,
former VP & GM, Global Consumer and Accountants, Global Business Division at Intuit

This book gives you the practical details you need to quickly ensure you and your product teams understand customers' needs and have organizational commitment much earlier, saving critical design and development time and allowing you to deliver more successful products. Most other product management books' proposals add complexity and process—Ms. Dinamani and Ms. Samarin refreshingly propose approaches that yield results in days and require few to no additional resources. I've immediately improved my teams' practices and only wish this book had been around in time for some of my past projects!

Jason Knapp ▪ Founder Strategic Data Corp,
former CPO at Myspace and Product Executive at Viasat

Product Rebels, Publisher
Cover design by David Miles
Interior design by Andrew Welyczko ▪ AbandonedWest Creative, Inc.
Book Production by Broad Book Group, LLC

ISBN-13: 9780578776323
eISBN: 9780578776330
Library of Congress Control Number: 2020919179

Printed in the United States of America

20 21 22 23 24 25   10 9 8 7 6 5 4 3 2 1

CONTENTS

PART I: THE GROUNDWORK

CHAPTER 1

CHAPTER 2

CHAPTER 3
GROUNDWORK PILLAR II: ACTIONABLE PERSONA

CHAPTER 4
GROUNDWORK PILLAR III: INDIVIDUALIZED NEEDS

PART II:
THE PRACTICES

CHAPTER 5
INTRODUCTION TO THE PRACTICES

FOREWORD

The strongest steel is forged in the hottest fires.

IN 2004, one of Intuit's flagship products, TurboTax, faced a moment
of truth. Years of feature-bloat, a rapid shift to web-based applications
and disruptive new competitors had converged to present a challenge the
brand had not experienced since its introduction. A company-wide call to
action ensued and I was tapped to participate in this effort as the General
Manager for the business. Fortunately, the company's commitment to right
the ship resulted in "elite athletes" from all areas of the company being
drafted and assembled to form the refreshed TurboTax team. It was at this
time that I was privileged to work closely with two of these elite athletes—
Heather (Crothers) Samarin and Vidya Dinamani, the authors of this book.

In the words of Leonard Bernstein, "to achieve great things, two
things are needed—a plan, and not quite enough time." That summed up
our circumstances in 2004 with one exception—we didn't have a plan.
What we had were symptoms to a problem and we needed to reground
ourselves in what mattered most—the customer.

While the clock ticked and the competition advanced, the team declared a return to our roots. We would rebuild deep empathy for the customer; fall in love with their problem and not our existing solution; develop multiple hypotheses for ways we might solve the problem better than existing alternatives (including our own); develop prototypes and run rapid experiments; treat success and failure as an opportunity to learn quickly; and ultimately narrow to a minimum viable product that would be measured in the only way that mattered—through the eyes of the customer.

The team tossed aside "vanity metrics" such as revenue and the number of customers, and refocused on the customer benefit delivered, active use, and the customer's willingness to recommend the product to friends and family (Net Promoter Scores). These metrics became known as the Love Metrics, because the end goal was to achieve unsurpassed customer delight. The efforts of the team righted the ship, the product returned to its innovative roots, and the franchise has accelerated in all measures of success since that time.

Perhaps the greatest outcome were the lessons learned, the principles developed and the market-tested approaches that have formed the foundation for what is explained in this book. Since that time, the authors have advanced the thinking, improved the framework and tested its success across many more companies and industries. What hasn't changed is the outcome this approach has produced time and time again. I am confident that the readers who make the effort to learn and apply the principles contained in this book will enjoy similar results to those of us who have battle-tested its effectiveness to-date.

Brad D. Smith ▪ Executive Chairman at Intuit

INTRODUCTION

WE MET back in 2004 at Intuit. At that time, Heather had come down to San Diego after launching and leading the QuickBooks Enterprise business in the San Francisco Bay area. She would now lead new product development for TurboTax and she was charged with launching a new offering within six months. Vidya had transferred from the CTO office to the tax business and in her new role she would lead business operations. Vidya was tasked with reducing customer contacts by 30% for the TurboTax product line. The previous year had been a difficult one for the company, with disastrous back-end failures for TurboTax. Consumers, competitors as well as the media came to see Intuit as lacking innovation, dull, and mediocre. We had our work cut out for us, as individuals, as a business, and as a company. It was also an inspiring time—full of hard work, failures, learning, and some spectacular successes.

We were both fortunate to sit on Brad Smith's[1] staff and learn from one of the best leaders in our industry. We also had frequent opportunities to learn from another great leader, Scott Cook[2]. Through Scott's strategic leadership Intuit developed into an innovation powerhouse. This meant that we had the opportunity to learn from leading thinkers throughout the country about the latest innovation theories and practices. We got to experiment, a lot. We developed our product muscles working for this amazing company and it instilled in us a specific way of thinking about and listening to customers. We left Intuit within a year of each other—joining separate companies as executives leading product and marketing departments—we focused on being able to build products faster and more effectively. Leveraging over a decade of experience working at Intuit, we experimented with different product delivery methods and processes to get to launch faster; we threw ourselves into lean startup principles and other forms of product delivery. We worked on a lot of products from consumer-facing to B2B, in industries as diverse as gaming to insurance. We hired a lot of product managers, grew teams and launched dozens of new products and features.

We kept in touch during the years when we were separately leading various product teams and shared what was working (and what to avoid!). We realized we shared a common priority passion: we both yearned for a repeatable approach that could quickly bring on new product managers and make them successful, without the one to two-year period it typically took to train and coach them. Because, in reality—that's what training product managers looks like. You hire smart people and then you work with them individually. You guide them through how to think about product management and you watch them develop. It's fun, but it takes so damn long to get them up to speed. We wanted a much faster way to cultivate efficient and effective product managers. When we figured out how to do it, we knew it had to work regardless of the industry, the environment, and the development methodology that the team employed.

---

[1] Brad later became CEO of Intuit from 2008-2018, and currently serves as Executive Chairman of the Board. At the time, he was GM of the TurboTax Division.

[2] Scott Cook is the esteemed co-founder of Intuit and currently serves as Chairman of the Executive Committee. He taught us so much about being customer-obsessed.

Our conversations to solve this centered on finding patterns and identifying the common elements of products we successfully built and launched and adopting them as standards to coach our teams in a consistent manner. We read treatises by the leading voices in the product management space and discussed and debated them. One of our favorite product gurus is Marty Cagan[3], who has been a thought leader in the craft of customer-driven product management for over a decade. We're big fans. We forced ourselves to review six-sigma-like product training, which focuses exclusively on process. Not big fans. And we looked both within and outside of the software industry for how successful product teams achieve outstanding results.

What we learned through our experience and research was that without preparing the right base for a product, *nothing else matters.* That's why we've called this book **Groundwork**.

You can have the best development teams and the smartest product managers (PMs) and it won't necessarily translate to delighted customers or company growth. You can be swimming in investment funds yet develop features that won't matter. You can constantly talk to customers and still not make customer-driven decisions. There are core decisions that form the foundation for your product, and these decisions go on to impact every metric that matters to a successful business: growth, revenue, retention, Net Promoter Score (NPS), engagement, sales, conversion, and so on.

So, why doesn't everyone pay close attention to these core decisions? The problem is that there are so many ideas about where to start and what's important, and everyone is eager to just start building—whether that's a prototype, a feature, or a new product. Even if everyone generally agrees that some level of product discovery and customer research are the best starting points, there are so many different approaches and methods to those two areas. We've tried a fair number of them ourselves. We've sent our teams off to training, approved travel to conferences far and near that promise to transform and elevate PM skills, brought in trainers to educate staff on the latest best practices. We've been infatuated with the

---

[3] One of our favorite product books is *Inspired* (Wiley, 2017)

latest management theories and bought the latest software that promised to speed up our teams and make their jobs easier. We've done all of this, just as you probably have. We're all in search of how to deliver products faster, more efficiently, with fewer workarounds, and with fewer decisions overturned.

Our Discipline Also Has A Few Strikes Against It

First, product management evolved out of business analysis, and was never a discipline with formal certification[4]. Product managers grow up in companies, sometimes they are pulled from marketing, customer service departments, or development. In some cases, project or program managers are expected to have product management skills, when there's never been an overarching authority providing guidance, or even guardrails. Consider that for every other department in a company—Finance, Development, HR, Design—people obtain degrees in the specific discipline. They review theories, learn best practices, and then they get hired to put into practice what they learned. Sure, each company requires individual flavors, but the core discipline offers a shared language and core understanding. No one invents their own way of developing a General Ledger.

This is not the case for product managers. Product managers come from all sorts of backgrounds. The lucky ones have grown up in a company that developed and shared their unique approach to product management or they benefited from product leaders that took the time to coach their teams consistently and continually. Every product manager learns on the job. Companies have a mix of well-meaning, smart, driven individuals who are doing the best they can, and each company approaches the practice of product management differently. They are measured based on the success of their product features; this creates a drive to build more and build faster.

The second strike is that we've been swept up in the wake of ever-changing product development practices. When waterfall development

---

[4] We're starting to see product management courses being offered at prestigious institutions like Kellogg, Cornell, and Berkeley. There's also a new degree in product management at Carnegie Mellon University.

was in vogue for product development, we wrote endless product requirements documents; with agile came the expectation of quickly produced user stories; we are even more severely challenged with Lean (or SAFe—we truly empathize if you're a product manager working within that framework). Whatever product development methodology you use, product managers must ensure that their development teams have work to do, so they go about creating a lot of work. Hence, a lot of products are simply bad—you may have used a few.

The third strike, and final nail in the coffin, is that all product managers like solving problems. Thinking about solutions excites and interests us much more than framing a problem correctly. Moreover, we're measured by output. Think about every performance review that you've received or have given. *Results count*, so we look to the work that's been delivered, neglecting to reward the thoughtful work behind the decisions that led to it. Doing the work to ensure that you're addressing the right problem is often unrewarding, leads to countless dead ends, and can be frustrating. It's no wonder we all jump to indulge in problem solving instead, and focus on keeping our development teams busy.

There's a lot working against us!

IN SEARCH OF BEST PRACTICES

We felt driven to define a set of basic principles to avoid so much wasted effort, that any product team can use—something that cuts through all the noise and opinions, based on proven team-oriented strategies. We looked hard at the product launches we had led, both successes and failures, and examined ours and others' products that were successful in the market. We talked with many teams nation-wide and found three elements that every successful product team and successful product had in common.

Every Team Had A Clear Problem to Solve

It didn't matter which direction they worked from—some teams began with a problem they could solve well and then sought to target the right customer; other teams began with a clear customer in mind and chose a problem they could solve well for that customer. Still other teams started with a great idea, and took the time to clarify the problem the idea solved and ensure the right path forward. All of these approaches worked equally well. But every successful team knew the problem and the customer before they ever considered how to solve the problem. They deliberately kept solutions at bay until they knew they had the right problem to solve for a particular customer, and they'd chosen an important enough problem that the customer was willing to pay for a solution to.

They Knew Their Customer Like the Back of Their Hand

The successful teams could tell you everything about their customer. They had true empathy, developed over many conversations with, and observations of their customer. It was evident that they knew their customer through the stories they shared readily with each other, and the artifacts the product team produced. Teams had materials highlighting their customers posted on their walls; the way they talked about their customer and what they could do for them showed that they'd really listened to their customer. Successful teams debated what mattered most to the customer based on evidence and not opinion. Every single person on the team understood the customer—not just the product manager or designer.

The Team Attached A Clear Set of Customer Needs to The Problem

We all know that every great product solves a problem better than the alternative. That's why we, as customers, pay for products. Teams that followed a method for learning and translating everything in and around that problem, including an intimate knowledge of their customers' environment and situational context, led to solutions that delighted the customer. This is what differentiated successful product teams from the rest. Regardless of how much (or little) customer research was done, teams that got this right showed the translation from what the customer did or said they wanted, to a focused set of product priorities that best met the needs of the target customer out of the starting gate. They could tell you what was most important to address first in the solution and why it was so important. They spoke in the language of customer needs, not features or ideas.

Based on these findings, we created some simple frameworks and templates around three areas: problem, customer, and needs. Then we started to test our paradigm outside of our product teams. We started by giving away dozens of free foundational workshops to early-stage companies. Those seeking every bit of help they could get, and in a position to benefit significantly from doing the work we recommended. We assumed most founders would never have worked in product management, but in a small startup, the founder/CEO owns the product, and drives all the key product decisions.

Our hypothesis was that if these non-product founders could learn the three fundamentals of problem, customer, and needs, they would be on the best trajectory for success. What was interesting was that we got to a stage where, within an hour, we could tell you which companies/founders "got it" and which would falter. All because they understood why the fundamentals were critical, and they knew they would have to go back to the drawing board to get the foundation right. Those that didn't get it would tell us the work was unnecessary, and wanted to jump straight to getting feedback on their features, or prototypes—asking our advice on marketing, teams or investment—and we knew they weren't ready. Through our own experience as product leaders, we know the same is true for any product team, big or small. We saw the pieces of our framework click into place while coaching those early-stage companies.

With our research and testing complete, we started working with bigger companies focused on software products, but also medical devices, life sciences, and services-based offerings. We kept testing and refining our approach to ensure our core foundation would work regardless of industry or type of product. In the last five years, we've had the opportunity to meet and coach hundreds of companies and we developed an online training program with a blended coaching model. With every company we work with—we use the Groundwork you'll read about here as the first step; as the basis to develop great product managers and successful products. We've worked across multiple industries from software, healthcare, and insurance, to direct-to-consumer. We know that paying attention to this foundation can dramatically change outcomes for a company, whether for a new company, a new product, a new feature, or a fix. We're certain that using our paradigm to approach all product work lets teams make lasting and impactful product decisions.

WHY WE WROTE THIS BOOK

The *problem we're solving* by writing this book is making product leaders confident that their product teams are consistently developing products that customers will buy and love. Product leaders who instill this foundation in every product team give their product a much higher chance of success in the market. They can set up their product managers for success. If this statement resonates, then this book is for you.

In these pages, we share the design philosophy and methodology behind *Groundwork*, and explain why it's so impactful and effective. We also share daily practices that strengthen your team's product management muscles necessary to establish the Groundwork successfully.

We're grateful to the many product leaders whose stories we share throughout this book. Their stories bring each chapter to life with real-world experiences. Some of these leaders we've worked with; we admire all of them. We all share a common philosophy around customer-driven product management, and hope these lessons illustrate the reason why the Groundwork should guide the way every product team chooses to work.

WHO THIS BOOK IS FOR

Do you lead a team with the primary goal of building experiences customers love? Do you get frustrated by seeing too many decisions overturned or delayed? Does your team have to do a lot of post-delivery rework of products or features? Have you ever said "Dang it! If we'd known that earlier, we would have done something different!"? If you've answered "Yes!" to any of these questions, this book is for you!

We wrote this book to teach product executives how to help their product teams succeed. Regardless of your industry or what type of product you offer, all product executives have one thing in common: You want happy customers who love your products. Happy customers tell others, they pay a premium, they buy more, and they stay loyal. We haven't met a company yet that doesn't want those things. And you want to work in a thriving environment, where employees are engaged, they understand the purpose of your company or product, and they remain loyal. Every company addresses these issues in a different way, but everyone shares these goals.

We wrote this book to help you establish a foundation that helps product teams and products thrive. We've kept it simple: There are three areas of focus that every product manager should understand thoroughly, and three practices that every product manager applies before they offer up a product idea, new product feature, or modifications to existing features. We wrote this book expecting that after you understand what's needed for your team to succeed, you will generously share these principles with your product teams. We want you to make sure your teams know that you expect them to follow the principles in *Groundwork* to make the team, the product and the company be successful. Changing or establishing foundational work can't happen bottom-up. They need you to lead, to follow through, and to hold them accountable.

Many of the scenarios in this book relate to software products. About 75% of the work we take on with clients is with teams who build software so we've drawn from these case studies and our personal experience in the industry. However, over the past four years, we've also applied the principles of *Groundwork* to clients who design manufacturing equipment, developing hardware, and designing service products. Our principles work for every product designed to be bought and used by a customer.

All that said, there are two groups of executives who we expressly wrote this book for: Product leaders and development leaders.

Product Leaders (Chief Product Officer, VP/Director Product Management, CEO)

Product Leaders, you're our tribe. We've been heads of product at many companies. We know how hard your job is, how hard your team works, and how overwhelming it is to connect the dots in every part of the organization to make your product successful. We know you're tired of being seen as project or program managers. We know you can't possibly keep up with every nuance of the product, market, competition, and technology. Yet you try. We get it. We wrote this book to make your job easier and more fun. Yes, fun.

It's so much more rewarding to help your team laser focus on the right problem to solve rather than run around with endless PowerPoint decks trying to get alignment from leaders in every department. It's more fun to watch the friction disappear as you set your teams up for success from the start, rather than run around fighting fires (externally and internally). It's so much more fun to ask the right questions, interact with customers, and make quick decisions that you know your team will support, rather than prepare for yet another battle. Maybe you'll establish the Groundwork in one team and test this for yourself? That's what we did.

A special note to our CEO founders: The reason the size of your company is unimportant is that regardless of a company's size, every product is created for a customer. Whether you have one product, or dozens, it's people that buy and use your product. You may have a complex series of decision makers, but ultimately your product solves a problem for a person. Whatever its size and impact, each of your products solves a problem. The better your product solves that problem, the more wildly successful it (and you) will be. Don't you want to know you nailed the problem before you invest in development, manufacturing, or clinical trials? Don't you want to minimize the time to launch? Don't you want confidence in product–market fit before you invest in marketing?

We want all these things for you too. The way you get there is by setting the expectation that anyone associated with producing your product is crystal clear on what they're building, who they're building it for, and why it matters to that customer. We will lay out exactly what it takes to achieve these things. As you read, ask yourself whether you see these activities happening in your organization. You may recognize some elements, but it's the combination of the work and the practices that lay a robust, fertile, and enduring foundation.

Development Leaders (CTO, VP/Director Development/Engineering)

To our wonderful peers in development: This book is for you, too. Especially those of you in engineering and technology.

Engineering Leaders. Particularly those who supervise frustrated, overworked, stressed out development teams complaining about the growing technical debt, and muttering that they have no idea why they're asked to rework the same feature for the hundredth time. The Groundwork will help you ask the right questions of your product team. As you go into sprint or release planning, challenge your product managers. Ask them to clearly identify the purpose of the development work (the "what"), so that you can bring together product and development to partner on solutions (the "how"). Set an expectation that the product manager must establish the Groundwork before they engage development teams with user stories (or requirements).

Technology Leaders who also lead product teams. That is, there isn't an executive product leader and all product owners report into your organization. Perhaps your entire background is technical and you're trying to figure out how to also lead the product team. We will guide you through the core product management practices you need to have in place before you set your development teams to work.

Finally, to anyone who doesn't fall into any of these categories but are curious about the Groundwork because they want to move into a product management role, or start a new company: we are not focused on you. This is a fairly technical book about adopting our product practices. We go into a lot of detail about the core areas needed to establish a product foundation and the core practices that support every aspect of a product management job. And while these aren't difficult to learn, they're best understood when you already have experience working in product management. If you don't have that experience and you'd still like to take this journey with us, think about a product you'd apply these practices to and then try them for yourself.

While the Groundwork takes discipline and practice, establishing the Groundwork in your organization immediately reduces product churn and increases team productivity, and with consistent application it will positively impact every business metric you care about.

UNDERSTANDING DELIGHT AND NPS

There are a couple of terms we use a lot in this book when talking about what it means to make better products. We started using the term "delight" back in our Intuit days to determine how well our products and features were received by customers. We weren't content to just measure customer satisfaction, we wanted to know if we had gone above and beyond expectations. The word "delight" has such a strong emotional pull, and there aren't many products that truly delight; it's a high bar.

The way that we chose to measure delight was through using the Net Promoter Score (NPS) methodology. There's been a lot written about NPS, and it's not everyone's favorite metric. However, we haven't yet found a better way to measure delight. The basic premise of NPS is understanding whether a customer will recommend your product (or service) to others. When you love using a product, you tend to tell others. And the converse is true. How many times have you complained about a product you hate? NPS simply asks you to score your likeliness to recommend the product or service on a scale of 0-10, and then asks one question, "Why did you answer that way?" We love the simplicity of the score and the question because it quickly and effectively captures a customers' sentiment, and the answer will give you an explanation to explore. We could write a whole book on delight and NPS, but for now just know that we use delight and NPS to measure whether you have truly built a better product for your customer.

USING THIS BOOK TO SURGICALLY ADDRESS SPECIFIC PROBLEMS

Each chapter is structured similarly so you can go straight to what you are looking for and bypass what you feel you already know or read it from cover to cover.

However, there are a couple of caveats.

We've purposely leveraged common terms—like *Convergent Problem Statement*, *Actionable Persona*, and *Individualized Needs*—because we believe that developing new jargon isn't as valuable as significantly improving how organizations operate in and around terms they already understand. That being said, we have a *very different definition* for each of these terms and made them significantly more actionable for you as a product leader. So be careful before assuming you have one of them mastered.

The three practices—*Developing Hypothesis*, *Conducting Scrappy Research*, and *Getting Commitment*—are the daily habits we want every great product leader to cultivate in their team. We recommend that in each chapter, you read at least the section on why the practice is so important. We also provide guidance in the way of tips and tricks on how to squeeze the most from your efforts.

We realize when product leaders pick up a book, they're often facing a specific challenge and are looking for help and immediate solutions. To address this, we highlighted the most common product leader challenges we encountered in our work with hundreds of product teams and recommended chapters you can skip to that will address the challenge.

Product Leader Challenge 1: I Am Drowning in New Ideas

This is probably the biggest challenge we see in business-to-business (B2B). A product leader struggles with a tremendous influx of ideas and "priorities" from all parts of the organization and their team struggles with the backlog and simple prioritization. We've all been there.

Here's what we usually find:

1. **No prioritization of users.** The problem space is pretty clear, but there are multiple target users who all seem equally important. These users haven't been prioritized or defined consistently across the business.
2. **No access to customers/clients.** The team doesn't have direct access to customers/clients because they're usually "protected" by the sales or account management team. This results in little or no customer interaction and learning, leaving the team translating what others say into possible ideas and solutions for problems they don't understand and impacts they can't quantify.
3. **No data-based decisions.** There is a consensus-driven organization, where everyone has a say, and therefore decisions feel more opinion-based than data-based.

Recommended Chapters to Read:

- **Groundwork Pillar II: Actionable Persona.** This chapter gives you a handle on who your most important targets are and defines personas in a way that allows for feature or idea tradeoffs.
- **Groundwork Pillar III: Individualized Needs.** This chapter helps you develop a clear set of prioritized needs by persona, facilitating justifiable tradeoffs between competing ideas, and saying no to shiny objects.
- **Practice II: Conducting Scrappy Research.** This chapter offers a practice to support your persona definition and needs prioritization efforts.
- *(optional)* **Practice III: Getting Commitment.** This chapter will help you facilitate effective tradeoffs to which the broader organization will actually commit. This is vital if you find that your decision-making process needs some help.

Product Leader Challenge 2: We Need to Innovate and Grow

All leaders hit this point in their career. The main product growth is slowing down, or business isn't growing as fast as planned, and you've been tasked with developing a strategy for growth.

Here's what we usually find:

1. **Can't penetrate new markets.** The company has been interested in a couple of target markets or problem spaces, but has made no real progress infiltrating them. There are lots of opinions within the leadership team circulating about how and where the company could grow.
2. **Strengthening the competition.** A new competitor is impacting your financials by undercutting your price, but cutting price isn't an option for you, so leadership wants new products and features to offer.
3. **Negative customer feedback.** It's harder to get customers, the team pours more money into marketing and sales, and customer

feedback suggests that there is less perceived value in what your products offer.

Recommended Chapters to Read:

- **Groundwork Pillar I: Convergent Problem Statement.** This chapter defines a few potential problems to test in the market and quantify opportunities.
- **Groundwork Pillar II: Actionable Persona.** This chapter gives you a handle on who your most important targets are within each problem space and defines personas in a way that allows for strategic tradeoffs.
- **Groundwork Pillar III: Individualized Needs.** This chapter helps you develop a clear set of prioritized needs by persona, facilitating the scope of prototypes to test.
- *(optional)* **Practice II: Conducting Scrappy Research.** This section offers a practice to support your groundwork efforts and helps set up quick prototype learning and evolution.

Product Leader Challenge 3: All I'm Doing Is Addressing Customer Complaints

We've gone into some companies where the list of bugs is overwhelming, customers are unhappy, and every support team is stressed out. You don't know where to start because you can't even get to new features until you fix the mess in front of you.

Here's what we usually find:

1. **Internal disagreements.** People in the organization have different definitions of the most important problem to solve and they constantly argue about where to focus.
2. **Too many options.** Team members aren't clear which customers are most important because the primary persona the product targets was never clearly articulated. So anything goes, so to speak.

3. **No prioritization processes.** No one has prioritized the set of needs for the primary personas, which means that understanding what's important is almost impossible; the loudest (or highest paid) voice wins.

Recommended Chapters to Read:

- One or both of the following:
  - ◆ **Groundwork Pillar I: Convergent Problem Statement.** This chapter helps you quickly agree on the problem(s) you are solving and quickly identify what to do differently. What do you cut? What do you add? What do you change? If your team is clear on the problem, then move to *Actionable Persona* instead.
  - ◆ **Groundwork Pillar II: Actionable Persona.** This chapter helps you agree on who your personas are and which ones to prioritize and, again, helps you identify what you would do differently.
- **Groundwork Pillar III: Individualized Needs.** This chapter helps you develop a clear set of prioritized needs by persona, facilitating further tradeoffs and potentially identifying areas where you can simplify the scope of the work.
- *(optional)* **Practice II: Conducting Scrappy Research.** This chapter introduces a fast way to learn from customers that supports all of the Groundwork Pillars: *Clarify the Problem, Define the Persona,* and *Uncover Needs.*

Some Additional Shortcuts

While those are some of the most common challenges, we address many more throughout the book. If you'd like to further focus your reading time, here are a few questions designed to guide you to a good starting point.

The Groundwork Pillars

1. **Groundwork Pillar I: Convergent Problem Statement.** *Are we all solving the same Problem?* If you asked your team what problem

a particular product effort solves and you're not 100% sure they'd say the same thing, or if your solution is part of the way you describe the problem, start here.

2. **Groundwork Pillar II: Actionable Persona.** *Have I Defined the Persona?* If the PM team (not your UX team!) hasn't used a persona to make a product decision in the last six months, start here.

3. **Groundwork Pillar III: Individualized Needs.** *Are we clear on Customer Needs?* Everyone should read this chapter. No exceptions.

The Practices

1. **Practice I: Developing the Hypothesis.** Was one of your last three research studies delayed due to lack of agreement on where to focus the customer learning or what questions to ask? If yes, then read this after any of the Groundwork Pillar chapters you complete.

2. **Practice II: Conducting Scrappy Research.** When was the last time you talked to your customer directly? If it wasn't last week, you must begin by reading this for inspiration.

3. **Practice III: Getting Commitment.** Have you had a product decision overturned in the last three months? Have you had a product decision delayed unnecessarily in the last three months? If the answer is yes to either of these questions, read this chapter.

Again, we hope you read the book cover to cover, but we know you're busy and we know that every product leader faces different challenges. We hope these shortcuts get you right to the point.

■ ■ ■

PART I

THE
GROUND
WORK

1

INTRODUCING
THE GROUNDWORK

WE NAMED this book *Groundwork* for a reason. The hard work to create a solid foundation for a product happens below the surface. It's not sexy, it's not showy, and it can get messy. It's no wonder most companies want to jump straight into developing and launching products—there's more instant gratification. But watch out for the pain of failure, which comes in the form of bad reviews, returned products, and poor sales. Some companies subscribe to rapid prototyping and launch a Minimal Viable Product (MVP) just to get to the endorphin high faster. Well, we're all for it *if* they've done the Groundwork. When they haven't, the MVP becomes just an excuse to get anything to market quickly and hope for the best. There's a better way that still strives for speed, but requires some upfront thinking. Not a ton of work—we want you to move fast as well—and we've done the Groundwork with teams in a matter of a few days, and sometimes even hours. This small investment of time will pay off in a big way.

The process we're going to teach you is indispensable to creating conditions that help a product take hold, flourish, and thrive. We're going to start by creating fertile ground with foundations that enable you to build your product with clarity and purpose. You can still launch a version 1, but if you've done the Groundwork, your entire dartboard becomes a bullseye.

The Groundwork consists of three Pillars (which we'll explore more later in this chapter):

1. **Convergent Problem Statement**
2. **Actionable Persona**
3. **Individualized Needs**

These three Pillars—Convergent Problem Statement, Actionable Persona, and Individualized Needs—are always in play beneath the surface of product ideas and product features. Each Pillar is critical; they work with, and build on each other, and each ensures that together, they support and harmonize with each other. Usually we start with understanding the problem or the customer, but there are cases where an unmet need is highlighted as a potential product idea. Wherever you start, make sure you address all three.

THE CASE FOR DOING THE GROUNDWORK

A great foundation sets up the conditions for your organization and team to build a great product. When you establish the Groundwork, you activate positive attributes for your team.

Prioritize More Easily

Let's face it, prioritization is one of the biggest challenges to any organization. The first thing every client we work with does is show us a laundry list of current, slated, and future ideas. Ideas are cheap, and most are worthless. But it's really hard to discern great ideas from poor ones by just thinking about them or endlessly talking about them. And when an idea comes from high up in the food chain, it gets assigned a premium value. Creating a foundation that we know will be right for certain types of products enables us to focus. We make decisions based on the unique foundation we build by understanding the customer, their conditions in which they work and live, and then prioritizing ideas that will thrive.

Say "No" Gracefully

There's nothing worse than making a decision about a product only to have it overturned a few weeks later for a new idea from the CEO, or as the result of the most recent compelling sales call, or because of a really unhappy important customer demanding action. Regardless of how compelling the idea might be, a strong foundation allows us to firmly and confidently say "No." With a strong foundation, we can explain why the conditions aren't right, and explain it with customer-backed data and rationale. We can separate the idea from the person who proposed it, and look at the idea simply on its merits: how well does it fit with our foundation? If there is a poor fit, then the answer will become obvious, and you won't be put in the position to have to say "No." If you still need to defend the "No," you are doing so with customer information, and not your opinion.

Create Stronger Product-Market Fit

Getting to product-market fit is the holy grail for all companies. Your product solves the customer need so well that they're paying for it. Doing the Groundwork gives you a deep understanding of the customer problem, a deep knowledge of your customer, and a way to translate what they say they want into what they actually need. Which means you know exactly what to build so that the customer will buy. Which translates into product-market fit. Aren't you convinced by now that the Groundwork will help you succeed?

Establish Teams that Commit

When teams understand both what they're doing and why they're doing it, they offer suggestions, they care, and they are more committed. In our experience, product managers who share the results from doing the Groundwork with their development teams increase overall team engagement significantly. You'll find that teams are inspired to offer feedback, alternative ideas, and even work overnight and weekends.

We've seen this happen again and again as a result of sharing how we built the foundation and the reasons why that foundation is important.

Become A Customer-Driven Organization

Companies spend a lot of time talking about how customer focus is so important. For those companies that actually do focus on the customer unrelentingly, it's in their DNA and they don't need to talk about it; they instinctively act that way. To become a customer-driven organization, you need to build a focus on the customer as you develop a product's foundation. If you create a fertile ground designed around your customer, your product will naturally meet their needs. Every product decision you make should be rooted in this foundation and you won't need to defend or explain the logic—it's obvious.

Reduce Opinion-Based Debates

Market, customer, and competitive data are all subject to interpretation to some extent and teams can argue about them. That's why they are not useful or successful as a basis for getting leadership commitment. In contrast, rallying around a customer and establishing a genuine understanding of their needs rallies an organization together. Everyone understands who their target customer is and what's important to that target customer. Discussions and debates turn to which strategy best meets the customer's needs, rather than which voice is loudest or carries the most weight.

THE GROUNDWORK PILLARS

The Groundwork Pillars are the foundation for building a customer-driven product management organization, and thus, for building customer-driven products. There are three Pillars that together makeup the Groundwork:

1. Convergent Problem Statement
2. Actionable Persona
3. Individualized Needs

Let's introduce each one.

Convergent Problem Statement

The very first step for any organization is to get clear on one problem they're solving. Don't laugh—you'd be shocked at how many well-established teams and organizations can't do this. The majority of products try to solve multiple problems and end up not solving any single problem exceptionally. How do you think products get all those bloated features? How often do you buy products based on a set of marketing promises and then get rid of them because you become so frustrated that the product didn't solve your problem?

In the **Groundwork Pillar I: Convergent Problem Statement** chapter, we describe what it takes to create a clear, compelling problem statement that you want to solve. One that accurately depicts the customer's problem in such a way that every single person on your team can understand, and it's clear that you have the right skills, technology and resources to successfully address the problem. This is ground zero for products. Nothing thrives without getting this right.

Actionable Persona

Customer personas get such a bad rap. We're talking about the stylized fictional character that is designed to represent a customer or segment. We've even contemplated using a word other than "persona," something more fun that readers won't dismiss so quickly. The problem with the concept of "persona" is that it got hijacked by big firms that made a lot of money, creating fancy personas for product teams that never used them. So now "persona" is the laughing stock of the product world.

Well, we're here to tell you that this foundational Pillar is critical, and we're going to show you the no-nonsense, absolutely free version that every product manager should embrace. Our version insists that the product manager closest to the customer creates the persona. That way product and business decisions are confidently made based on your persona. Our persona is not pretty, it's a workhorse. Our lofty goal is that the Actionable Persona makes you rethink your entire opinion of personas and you can't wait to develop one that represents your customer. In any case, you can't complete the Groundwork without it.

Individualized Needs

The last Pillar to build the Groundwork is Individualized Needs, and it's the third step required before you can merrily start thinking about product solutions, roadmaps, or features. Everything you learned about the problem and the customer translate to customer needs. Needs aren't requirements and they're not user stories. They are your insights based on observation and interaction with your customers. We call them Individualized Needs because they are connected very specifically to your Actionable Persona. When you stratify needs, you can make priority calls. Whatever you build, create, or manufacture is rooted in understanding what will best satisfy a specific customer need.

In our experience, customers forgive incomplete and even (we're embarrassed to admit) buggy products as long as the product meets their primary need. The most loyal customers in every company we've worked with became promoters of the products. Without receiving a penny in compensation, they share their love for our products because our product solved their most important *individual* needs. Isn't this what each of us wants for our products? That they solve a real need (and the free, enthusiastic promotion is quite nice, too).

SUMMARY

We will describe each Pillar of the Groundwork in more detail, share how to build each Pillar, and explain exactly how to use each Pillar to create a step-by-step guide to establish the Groundwork successfully. We'll share some cautions, so that you can build each Pillar with guardrails that warn of common mistakes so you avoid getting yourself hurt. We'll also share stories from product leaders of some great companies. And lastly, we share what it looks like when you get it right to give you clarity and inspiration.

As a leader, you must set the expectation that the Groundwork is expected from every product manager before they present any early product work such as design sketches or prototypes. Each chapter shows you how to ask the right questions to focus your team on the *what* and *why* before they ever jump into the *how*.

The Groundwork can seem deceptively simple. And yes, this can be done in hours if your team is well-versed in the customer. You could be on your merry way after one working session. We've developed the Pillars such that you could use them immediately. For others, the first time you use this approach, the results may feel rocky. That's okay. In that case, be okay with iterating several times. Be patient. The results get radically better with each iteration, and with each iteration your team gets better at understanding the customer problem, building empathy with your customer, and prioritizing the customer needs, all of which sets the ideal Groundwork for your product to thrive.

■ ■ ■

2

GROUNDWORK PILLAR I: CONVERGENT PROBLEM STATEMENT

LET'S START by defining the problem. Think back to the last three major product initiatives you or one of your team members drove; pick a project that was especially impactful for revenue or the company's strategic positioning. Which option below sounds more like your team's path to development?

> **Option 1:** *The initiative started with someone's great idea. We discussed, scoped, and tested the idea. We then evolved the idea a bit, wrote detailed requirements and a design, and kicked off development.*

> **Option 2:** *The initiative started with someone's great idea. We then stepped back to validate that the idea solved a problem the customer had. We spent time defining the problem in more detail and made sure it was a problem we wanted to solve, and that*

our team and company were in a position to solve the problem well. We tested different prototypes of the solutions until we found the one the customer would pay for. We then created set requirements along with a design and kicked off development.

Although both options are valid and can result in success, Option 1 holds a much higher likelihood of delay and rework. Once an idea takes root in the form of a solution, it's hard to let it go. When we teach design thinking, we refer to this as the time-love continuum—the longer you spend thinking and discussing a single idea, the more you fall in love with it. The danger with Option 1 is that we hold onto the idea and try to perfect the solution.

Going straight to a solution makes sense; after all, human brains evolved to solve problems, and once we see a problem, we want to go straight to figuring out how to fix it. We get excited about the solution we invent and want to *tell everyone* how extraordinary it is. We become infatuated with our exquisite, elegant solution. We convince our team, our management, and our investors that our idea is brilliant. We keep going (and going), build more (and more), and pour money into marketing, because we believe that if we just get the product finished and the messaging just right, customers will flock to it. CEOs, founders, product leaders—we're all guilty of this mistake. We work in this field because we excel at understanding problems, quickly figure out how to resolve them, and deliver solutions. Those of us who are successful are extremely effective at persuading others that they're on the right path. Option 2 is radically different because it takes the focus off the idea/solution, and turns our attention towards understanding the problem.

Sounds simple doesn't it? The first step to building great products is to describe a problem that matters; a problem that customers experience and are willing to pay to eliminate. But so many companies, and the majority of startups we've worked with, tend to *start with a solution* and skip the critical step of defining the problem so that everyone in their company understands the problem that needs to be solved.

What's usually accepted as the first step in any idea for a new product or major new feature is something called *product–market fit*, a phrase first coined by Andy Rachleff[5] who said:

A value hypothesis is an attempt to articulate the key assumption that underlies why a customer is likely to use your product. Identifying a compelling value hypothesis is what I call finding product/market fit. A value hypothesis identifies the features you need to build, the audience that's likely to care, and the business model required to entice a customer to buy your product. Companies often go through many iterations before they find product/market fit, if they ever do.

We agree with much of what Andy says here. Establishing a core value hypothesis—which requires understanding the audience and their willingness to pay—is fundamentally what we see as the best practice for developing products. But starting with the product–market fit misses one critical factor. It assumes that you already have done the work to understand the problem, and therefore the *value hypothesis* that Andy refers to is then a matter of iterating features and enticing the right customer. We don't want you to ever start with identifying features, we want you to start with identifying problems. You should only start thinking about features (solutions) after you've identified a specific problem. There's one more assumption that we'd like to address: Getting to a successful product-market fit assumes that you know the core customer problem intimately and that you have your entire team on the same page. Making these assumptions is what leads so many companies to leap ahead to identifying features and to start testing prototypes with customers. But this process will not help you build a product that customers will love.

In one of our early workshops we had two co-founders who were trying to "pivot" their product roadmap (another of our not-so-favorite words, it's usually just trading one set of bad features for another set of bad features). They had been working together for two years, had built a product, and launched with some early sales. But then sales dramatically slowed and they struggled to get current customers to renew. They came

---

5 Andy Rachleff teaches courses on technology entrepreneurship at Stanford. He co-founded Benchmark Capital and invested in companies such as eBay, OpenTable, and Uber.

to our workshop hoping that we'd review their roadmap and help them make some key priority calls (which set of features shall we swap around?) that would get them to a product–market fit. Whenever we introduce defining the customer problem as our first step, it's usually met with smiles and knowing looks and statements like, "Well, this is easy!" But when our clients try to write out the problem, they find it's not so easy.

We asked these particular co-founders to write problem statements for their products, separately, without talking to each other. Then they shared them. As they read their statements to each other, they found that they had written very different problems from one another. Essentially, they were trying to solve two different problems with their product, because *they'd never discussed what problem they were trying to solve.* Each of the problems they'd written down was viable, but would require very different solutions to meet customer needs. No wonder they couldn't agree on what to build next. Their current feature set wasn't optimized for either of the problems, so no wonder their sales had slowed; they weren't solving any one problem well. No wonder customers were confused and not wanting to renew. No amount of marketing dollars would help.

This happens time after time. When we ask teams to write down the problem they're solving, they find enormous gaps in understanding. A majority of the problems they write down tend to be based on assumptions. After reading the next few sections, ask each core member of your team to fill out the Convergent Problem Statement Template we share on page 24. It shouldn't take more than 5-10 minutes to find out if the members of your team are aligned around the same problem. Do they understand what core problem your product is solving?

One last note about problem statements: We emphasize this so strongly because when you and your teams don't get the problem right, teams go through iteration after iteration of a product or feature, searching in vain for that magic moment when the "market really wants your product." You end up with products that customers won't buy (at least not at the level you expect) and overly busy customer service departments dealing with confused and unhappy customers. You see mediocre product reviews and deal with unengaged teams. These are just some of the symptoms you encounter when you omit the work needed for Groundwork Pillar I:

Convergent Problem Statement. Don't take our word for it, here's Marc Andreessen[6]:

> *You can always feel when product/market fit isn't happening.*
> *The customers aren't quite getting value out of the product, word*
> *of mouth isn't spreading, usage isn't growing that fast, press*
> *reviews are kind of 'blah', the sales cycle takes too long, and lots*
> *of deals never close.*

The root cause of all of this unhappiness is a lack of a clear problem statement. Start with step zero before going to product-market fit. Insist on defining one **problem statement** that you carefully select. This approach works whether you have a complex product line or a single product; it works whether you are changing features for an existing product or adding new features.

WHAT IS A CONVERGENT PROBLEM STATEMENT?

People don't want a quarter-inch drill, they want a
quarter-inch hole.

This quote, attributed to Harvard professor Theodore Levitt, is usually invoked in the context of sales and marketing. Understand what a customer needs but may not realize they need, and then sell them on that need by speaking to the customer in terms of benefits, rather than features. This is great, but it fails when the product doesn't deliver on the benefits in the first place. If the product doesn't deliver on the benefits, buyers feel letdown, or worse, taken advantage of. Great marketing works when the product meets the need. So how do you gain an understanding

---

[6] Marc Andreessen is a well known entrepreneur and investor. He was the co-founder of Netscape, and currently is the co-founder and general partner at the venture capital firm Andreessen Horowitz.

of the need? Going back to the quarter-inch drill/hole quote, let's take a closer look at what the actual customer problem might be. Let's take away the immediate need to sell more drills or drill bits, and think about what the customer is trying to do.

- **What is the quarter-inch hole for?**
  What are they going to do with this hole?
  ↳ Maybe they're trying to hang a picture…
    Well, what type of picture?
  ↳ Maybe it's a wall calendar, or a 20-pound canvas?
  ↳ Where are they trying to hang it?
  ↳ Is this in their home, or do they need the quarter-inch hole made in a brick wall at their industrial office space?

You can see that there are many possible reasons this quarter-inch hole is needed. Even when we move away from wanting to sell drills and we focus on an outcome; we still don't know *why* a customer wants that outcome. Note that as we asked questions, we didn't once mention a drill (or drill bits). All of the questions focus on what the customer is *trying to do*.

Problem statements are rooted in understanding your customer, which comes from watching and talking to the customer. You'll discover many problem statements when you're doing any customer research. A convergent problem statement clearly describes the most relevant difficulty the customer is dealing with and is stated with no attempt to address possible solutions.

WHAT A CONVERGENT PROBLEM STATEMENT IS NOT

Before we continue, a few words on red flags you should watch out for when you, or your team, are creating a problem statement. If you see these yell, "Danger! Danger!"

It's Not Circular in Logic

The biggest trap that teams get into when writing any problem statement is that they build their solution right into the problem. It goes something like this: "The problem exists because you don't have my product." Believe it or not, this is an easy trap to fall into. To avoid this, try defining the customer's problem as if your product will never exist. Do you understand what the customer is trying to do? Or are there some aspirational hopes in there, linked directly to the features you hope to sell? Our acid test is to check and see if there is anything that resembles a feature in the statement. If there is, start again.

It's Not Biased

It's easy to bring hope into your problem statements. Staying neutral and looking at the situation through an objective lens is critical. State the problem as it exists, not how you wish it to exist. Don't exaggerate the conditions. Pretending the customer has a problem (or the problem is worse than it actually is) will not make it magically so. The best way to test for this red flag is to ask someone outside your immediate work circle to read your problem statement. If you wrote a proper statement, it should make sense to a neutral party. If you find yourself explaining or defending it, go back to the drawing board.

It's Not Missing a Person

Our problem statement starts with "who" because we want to identify with a single person, or perhaps a role to create empathy. Be careful not to think this problem impacts "everybody," because *everybody* is an impossible customer to delight. The more specific you are regarding the person who's impacted by the problem, the more targeted and specific your solution will be. Remember, this is paint-by-numbers, not broad abstract art.

It's Not About Symptoms

The fourth leading cause of problem statement failure is talking about symptoms instead of root cause. A symptom is a clue but it's not the driving problem. This shows up mainly when we ask about barriers and root cause. Most products have alternatives, possibly poor ones, but they do exist. The only way to understand why this problem exists for a customer is to keep asking why until you're exhausted. Channel your inner three-year-old and keep going until you get to the truth. It's out there.

It's Not Vague

Make sure the problem statement isn't generic. It should be fairly clear about what you're not going to do because you're specific and detailed about what you're going to solve. This red flag is usually pretty easy to spot, because the problem will feel way too high level.

WHY IS A CONVERGENT PROBLEM STATEMENT IMPORTANT?

The problem statement is the first step in the Groundwork because it sets the stage for everything the product is and will do. A complete problem statement addresses several key points to help with your overall product strategy.

Get Your Product Hired

We're big fans of Clayton M. Christensen[7], and his concept of "jobs to be done," and we happily borrow this term. Think about your product doing a job for someone: A customer hires your product and they expect it to deliver a benefit. When we hire people, we look at their experience (features), we talk to their references (testimonials) and we discuss salary (price). If they all match our needs, we hire them (purchase).

To hire the right person, we write a job description. If we need a developer, we're not going to look for someone with a fantastic degree from a great school who can be an incredible marketer. A problem statement is the job description for your product stated in a way that demonstrates a deep understanding of the customer's problem. When the problem statement matches the customer's needs, they will hire your product.

---

[7] Clayton M. Christensen was a professor and consultant who wrote *The Innovator's Dilemma* (Harvard Business Review Press, 2016) and introduced the term "Disruptive Innovation." We were lucky enough to learn directly from him when we worked at Intuit.

Let's take a small detour. Here's how Christensen describes the "jobs-to-be-done (JTBD)":

> *The jobs-to-be-done point of view causes you to crawl into the skin of your customers and go with her as she goes about her day, always asking the question as she does something "why did she do it that way?"*

We love this quote for so many reasons. It evokes a picture watching a customer, not just at one moment of time, but in the context of her day, taking the time to deeply understand her. Our methodology is rooted in exactly this type of deep understanding. Not a survey or focus group, but actually doing the leg work of following your customer around. "Why?" should be the most overused question in any product manager's lexicon. You should be continually getting to root causes, and not be satisfied until you find a satisfactory explanation for why the customer behaves as she does.

There's a lot already written about JTBD and we think it's best you read from the author who coined the term. For large teams charged with innovation, JTBD is often a useful methodology for product discovery. However, for most product teams, it's an overly heavy methodology requiring too much time—a commodity most product managers don't have. Instead, we believe that you should take the meaning and intent of JTBD and apply it to every research step. This way you're always thinking in terms of someone hiring your product to fulfill a need. With this mindset, you can change the way you think about your product from addressing one-off isolated situations to continually considering the way in which your product is used as the person goes about their day.

The easiest way to execute the JTBD methodology is to simply focus on the "*Why?*" Dig into the underlying tasks your customer is trying to accomplish and keep asking "*Why?*" until you focus on a single compelling customer problem.

Focal Point for Strategy

The right convergent problem statement exists as the focal point for your business strategy. After all, you're in business to deliver a solution to an important customer problem, and do so in a way that's better than anyone else can. Once you clearly understand the problem, you can develop a multiyear strategy to deliver. The heart of your strategy is your deep understanding of the problem you're solving—not what the competition is doing, and not what your CEO (or investor) dreams up as the next amazing product. That may be a bit harsh, but we've seen so many product backlogs filled with ideas that product teams tell us came from senior execs. Don't put anything on your roadmap or backlog without a problem statement. It's a great disinfectant for random thoughts.

Focal Point for Ideation

We just said that you don't want random acts of inspiration because they lead to adding products or features that no one will buy. But we also said to develop a strong Convergent Problem Statement, because it is the best way to start ideation or brainstorming. After the entire team understands the *core problem* to solve, that's when you want wild and crazy ideas, sharply focused on how to solve that single problem. We've participated in a lot of ideation sessions that encourage thinking broadly, "think outside the box!" But, without a specific problem to focus on, all ideas have some merit and choosing one idea over another feels random. That's one of the reasons so many people opt out of ideation sessions: they feel like futile exercises. Before we run any ideation sessions, we make sure we set up a compelling problem statement rooted in customer understanding. We show why and how we selected the chosen problem statement from the alternatives. This way, our teams understand the context and rationale and they get excited about solving the real problem.

Easy Product Tradeoffs

Once you have a Convergent Problem Statement, product and feature tradeoffs are so much easier. Rather than argue the merits of one product feature over another, or consider what your organization is capable of, you start with one simple question: How well does this idea solve the customer's problem? Start with every feature that rates highly on solving customer problems, then introduce factors such as difficulty of developing the solution, costs, resources, etc. We always ask teams to first prioritize each feature's impact on how well it solves the problem, and only then discuss how each feature impacts the product (e.g., roadmap, resources, timeline), the business (e.g., growth, revenue, NPS), and the technology (e.g., architecture, resources, technical debt). You'll have a much shorter list to review when you begin with that one simple question: How well does this idea solve my customer's problem?

Enable Decisions

Every software product team we've ever worked with has an exploding backlog of initiatives, features, and customer issues they want to address someday. For non-software companies, the equivalent of a backlog is a long list of everything that the company wants to do. That's because we need somewhere to store new product ideas, customer-reported issues, potential features, etc. It's the list of technical debt that's been accumulated—we don't want to lose anything, so we keep a list of every possible area their company or product could possibly address. And most teams work on only the top 1 to 5% of this list, if that. Focusing your first decision criteria around how well a product solves a customer's problem drives your ability to make a faster, more impactful decision. The closer your product comes to solving a customer's core need, the better your chances of getting your product hired.

Stop the Interpretation Madness

Most of the time when your team argues about the product roadmap, or feature prioritization, it's because they're making assumptions that they aren't articulating. As we pointed out earlier with the example of the two co-founders who were solving significantly different problems, unarticulated assumptions are pretty common. Each team member brings their own interpretation of what's important to the customer and the business unless you make sure they're all on the same page. This is why it's important to identify which customer problem you're solving, and to solve only one at a time.

To summarize, a Convergent Problem Statement articulates the reason for your product's existence. Take the time to create one before you start creating features or finding a product-market fit.

ELEMENTS OF A CONVERGENT PROBLEM STATEMENT

Let's examine what goes into our Convergent Problem Statement. We want to clearly define the problem in detail so that anyone reading the problem statement can immediately understand the situation. Every problem statement should address the following six questions.

1. Who Does It Impact?

You need to be able to imagine the person impacted by the problem. In the next chapter, Groundwork Pillar II: Actionable Persona, we'll delve deeper in understanding the customer, but for now, let's start by at least defining a real human being—someone you can relate to. Developing a sense of the person who has the problem immediately creates a sense of empathy. This empathy allows us to better understand the problem. Don't focus on demographics; think about a specific person in a particular role. You don't need to name them, but you do want a sense of who they are, where they work, and what their day-to-day life might look like.

2. What Are They Trying to Do?

Using our earlier example about the quarter-inch hole, we want to understand the context in which the person is operating. Here you'll think in more depth about where they live, or work, or play. Their surroundings matter. You need to know what they have access to, what their environment looks like and what options are available for them. You start to build a picture of what they have access to, the workarounds or options they may consider to naturally approach the problem.

3. How Do They Want to Feel?

We love this question. Yes, it's touchy-feely, but it goes to the core of why someone will care about the problem being solved. And for all you super-analytical types, this will be a cornerstone as you think about marketing. Understanding the emotional toll of the problem will help you sell the benefits of using your product. Every problem in your life leads to an emotion.

When the person you envision experiences the problem at hand, do they feel annoyed? Grumpy? Frustrated? Angry? Exhausted? This is one of the hardest questions to answer, so keep exploring different adjectives until you find the one that resonates. When you land on the right emotion, it will feel like an "aha!" moment. Understanding how your customer feels can reveal whether the problem is a serious or a trivial one. Asking these emotion questions help you determine the list of features needed to solve the problem, how to develop the solution, and how to price it. But let's not jump ahead of ourselves; there's still more to learn about the problem.

4. What's Getting in the Way of Just Addressing the Problem?

When customers have problems, they've usually tried to address them in some way if it's important enough. Have they tried alternative solutions? Did anything partially work? Have they created workarounds, whether that's through supplementary software or manual steps? Have they tried to reduce the impact of part of the problem? What are the biggest barriers to resolving their problem? Is it lack of awareness? Budget? Time? This question asks you to both ask direct questions, and also to closely observe behavior and actions.

5. When Does This Problem Occur?

This question is about timing. Is this a recurring problem? Is it a daily or a weekly problem? Does it only occur at the end of a fiscal quarter? Or does it occur once, but when it occurs, is it extremely painful? Understanding the frequency of the problem gives you a sense of the scale and size of the problem. This question pushes innovative thinking; understanding what's happening for the customer at different points of time allows us to consider alternatives.

6. Why Does This Problem Exist?

As you complete the problem statement, start to develop a hypothesis about why this particular problem exists for your customer. What gets in the way of just going about their day and avoiding this problem? Are there any alternative solutions or products that are just not viable, or is there no solution and they are creating a set of workarounds? Try not to go straight to willingness to pay for a solution as the answer, after all, people will pay a lot to solve an important problem. Instead, consider other factors that might be causing this problem. Remember, it's for the particular person that you imagined in the first question (who does the problem impact?). Don't generalize across a population to determine why the problem exists.

The answers to these six core questions paint a picture of your customer and their problem. Start the process by filling in the blanks in the Convergent Problem Statement Template below:

FIGURE 2–1

Who?
↳ PERSON / JOB TITLE

wants to
↳ ACHIEVE WHAT?

and needs to feel
↳ AN EMOTION / STATE OF BEING

but they can't achieve this due to
↳ WHAT'S GETTING IN THE WAY? WHAT'S THE TOP BARRIER IN ACHIEVING A RESULT?

which happens when
↳ TIMING

because
↳ ROOT CAUSE OF PROBLEM

While this template looks kind of awkward, (and we highly recommend you don't go around talking like this to anyone outside the product team) we'll show you how to translate this into a sentence that you can share later with your team and within your company. But these questions are critical to nail down. Each "fill-in-the-blank" section contains critical information for the product manager, and it takes time to get the answers right. Within a product team, these questions should become instinctive; they are the questions you should ask of yourself, and people within your team. If you can't fill in this template with confidence, don't bother trying to build something. What you'll find is that you'll iterate as you learn more about your customer, and you'll converge to a single statement that defines the problem.

A PRACTICAL EXAMPLE

Now that you have the elements of the problem template, let's see how it works by revisiting our drill bit problem. Imagine a situation where a quarter-inch hole is needed:

A person living in a condo wants to hang pictures on their wall.

This statement can be seen as a high-level problem. Now, let's assume we went to visit some condominiums. Let's use what we observed and learned, and complete our Convergent Problem Statement Template for our problem statement. We've developed these two problem statements for two different customers:

FIGURE 2–2

A

↳ RENTER

wants to

↳ HANG PHOTOS

to feel like

↳ THEIR SURROUNDINGS ARE MORE PERSONAL

but they can't because of

↳ STRICT RENTAL POLICIES ABOUT NOT DAMAGING ANY WALLS

which they learn when

↳ THEY MOVE IN AND SIGN THEIR RENTAL AGREEMENT AND AGREE TO ENFORCED PENALTIES FOR ANY DAMAGE

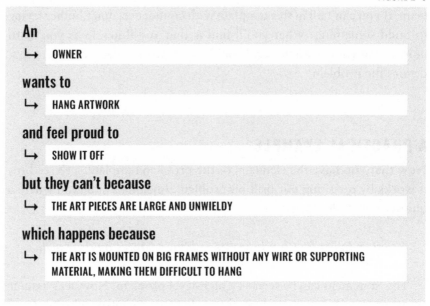

An

↳ OWNER

wants to

↳ HANG ARTWORK

and feel proud to

↳ SHOW IT OFF

but they can't because

↳ THE ART PIECES ARE LARGE AND UNWIELDY

which happens because

↳ THE ART IS MOUNTED ON BIG FRAMES WITHOUT ANY WIRE OR SUPPORTING MATERIAL, MAKING THEM DIFFICULT TO HANG

Could a quarter-inch hole be the solution to each of these? Probably not. But we bet you immediately thought of different solutions as you read each of the problem statements. These two different problem statements solve for different customers with very different needs. The problem you choose to focus on now depends on your team's capabilities, your business goals, competitor offerings, the market, and other factors. You converge on the problem you wish to go after by developing the statements in detail and then making a deliberate choice.

The Convergent Problem Statement puts you in a position to consider alternatives and open yourself up to problem solving. A great problem statement is the precursor to effective ideation. Asking a team to deliver the equivalent of a quarter-inch hole without knowing why or who they're making it for is the killer of creativity. Yet, that's what so many product managers do when they write *requirements*[8], instead of sharing the problem. When the product manager gives developers a set of instructions, it's like building IKEA furniture with no pictures, no clear instructions,

---

[8] We use the word requirements loosely. This can include user stories, a more formal product requirements document, or even technical specifications.

and no view of the end product. Who knows what you'll end up with—sure it's furniture, but it's quite unlikely to be the item you wanted. And think of all that time wasted trying to interpret bad instructions.

This is why we often start the Groundwork with the Convergent Problem Statement. You need to be crystal clear about what the underlying problem is, who you're solving it for, and why. Once you have these elements in place, you have a clear starting point for thinking about solutions. You can invite people to help think about the many creative ways to address the problem. You can take a look at the business assets you have, the technical know-how, the partnerships, and the infrastructure in which you do business. You're optimally prepared to start solutioning.

HOW TO DEVELOP A GREAT CONVERGENT PROBLEM STATEMENT

Let's have some fun with our Convergent Problem Statement. Can you guess what existing product this statement represents?

FIGURE 2–4

A
↳ FREQUENT BUSINESS TRAVELER

wants to
↳ EASILY ACCESS ALL THEIR TRAVEL INFORMATION

and needs to feel
↳ ORGANIZED AND PREPARED

but they can't achieve this due to
↳ MULTIPLE DIFFERENT TYPES OF TRAVEL INFORMATION

which happens when
↳ THEY BOOK PLANES, HOTELS, AND CARS FROM DIFFERENT VENDORS

because
↳ EACH VENDOR SENDS INFORMATION IN A DIFFERENT FORMAT

Did you guess TripIt? They nailed the problem of organizing back in 2006 when multiple travel sites gave frequent travelers completely different kinds of information and we simply couldn't keep track of all the documents. Travelers were confronted with a change because what used to be done by a travel agency (organize all the travel plans in one document) was now in their hands, and they were overwhelmed. TripIt's wonderfully simple solution was to have business users forward their itineraries to the app, and the app magically organized information from all the different documents into one simple view.

TripIt was an instant win because it solved this one key problem so well and so simply. They did this so successfully that they were acquired in 2011 by Concur, a well-known SaaS organization. Interestingly enough, last year TripIt announced a refresh. Their team shared that they wanted to expand their product beyond planning and organizing just the beginning of the trip, but wanted to help organize every stage of the trip including reward program trackers, baggage claim info, and even expense reports. They retained the initial critical step of supporting the planning stage, which means they stay true to the original customer problem, but now help travelers during the trip and all the way to returning home. They also expanded their focus from business travelers to serve all types of travelers, including leisure travelers.

With more competition from other travel organizations offering similar services, we're watching to see whether this expanded focus resonates with a broader group of customers. We like that they stayed true to their initial problem statement and the core of the product still helps put disparate travel documents together with ease.

Are you ready to try this for your product? Fill in this template with specific information about your product and customer.

◆ ◆ ◆

The first step of the Groundwork looks deceptively easy—it's not. Getting the Convergent Problem Statement right requires hours of discussion and multiple iterations. It's not unusual to update and refine a product statement over a dozen times as we converge towards a single compelling problem. In coaching clients, we will often spend 2-3

FIGURE 2–5

Who?

↳ PERSON / JOB TITLE

wants to

↳ ACHIEVE WHAT?

and needs to feel

↳ AN EMOTION / STATE OF BEING

but they can't achieve this due to

↳ WHAT'S GETTING IN THE WAY? WHAT'S THE TOP BARRIER IN ACHIEVING A RESULT?

which happens when

↳ TIMING

because

↳ ROOT CAUSE OF PROBLEM

weeks with teams working on multiple product statements, pulling out assumptions and validating those with customers and prospects, working to ensure we have adequate proof points to support their statements. We look for evidence that our problem statement is right through customer interviews, or market research, or talking with internal teams who interact with customers. We're looking for the most relevant problem statement that's worthy of our focused attention. After all, if you're going to spend many months building your product, don't you want to make sure you are solving the right problem? Here are some tips on how to make developing a problem statement easier.

Understand Your Customer

Nothing beats having a really strong understanding of who you are solving the problem for. With TripIt, for example, we said "frequent business travelers," which is very specific. When you think about business travel, you think about someone trying to get somewhere quickly, with a purpose. This isn't for people going on leisurely, pleasant trips for fun;

frequent business travelers need to get somewhere efficiently. Nor is it for occasional business travelers, who may think of travel as a fun getaway from the office, or who aren't bothered by occasionally organizing things for themselves. TripIt's frequent business travelers are the people at the airport who pay for CLEAR because every minute counts and waiting in lines is a dreadful waste of time. It's important to get as specific as possible and uncomfortably narrow in the depiction of a customer because that specificity helps drive the clearest understanding of the problems they deal with.

Watch Customers in Their Environment

We'll talk a lot more about watching customers in the Practice II: Conducting Scrappy Research chapter, but know that it's critical to watch customers in their habitat. In the TripIt example, you might have a hypothesis about (or experienced yourself) the hassle of trying to set up travel plans. But you must watch business travelers from the minute they realize they need to go somewhere, to see how they merge various plans together. What works well and what causes frustration or anxiety? Go with them as they head to the airport or train station—what documents do they need? Where are those documents stored? How easy is it to locate the information as they start their travel, when they land, when they arrive at a hotel? As you can see, we're immersing ourselves in the environment the customer lives in. You may find you have several problem statements. Perhaps there's one focused on common failure points like missing flights, which causes multiple downstream issues. Or perhaps you focus on how much time it takes to plan all the different travel and keep it within a budget. When it comes to a broad topic like travel, you'll undoubtedly uncover many different possible problems. In the event that you have multiple problem statements that all equally meet important customer needs, we turn to our team capabilities, competitor offerings, and market data to understand which problem statement makes the most business sense to follow.

Identify the Job

Remember, you want your product to be hired to do a job. In the absence of your solution, what does the customer currently do to work around the problem? Before TripIt, the customer used manual labor. Every document needed to be printed or stored electronically and then organized. Travelers had to open calendars and enter details for each step of a trip. They had to cross-reference documents to avoid overlapping travel commitments, or to build in time to get from one airport to another. TripIt replaced boring, tedious, and annoying manual labor, and we were willing to hire their product to do the jobs we didn't want to do.

Check for Hidden Solutions

Review your problem statement for any hidden solutions. They sneak in there, especially when we feel we understand the problem and want to jump to the solution. Make sure the problem exists without any trace of your company or product. This is our acid test of a strong problem statement— when we can see several different ways that very different companies with different resources might go about addressing the problem. When this is the case, we can move to how our client can uniquely solve the problem in a way that they're uniquely positioned to succeed.

The Team Test

The best way to determine if you've written a great problem statement is to share with others: we call this the team test and we make it a part of every meeting for the teams that we coach. We ask what new problem statements they have uncovered. We have the team read the statements aloud. This practice often helps product managers refine their thinking. It also allows teams to offer feedback, helping drive the precision and clarity of the problem statement. As a product leader, you need to set the expectation that no work starts without a shared understanding of the problem.

The Gut Check

As you choose the final Convergent Problem Statement, check it against all your planned initiatives—does your Convergent Problem Statement feel at least as exciting as the work you're already considering? Does anything fall off the initiatives list because it's less important than pursuing this new problem? If all the work you had originally planned to do is still there, then your problem statement is not compelling enough of a problem to go after. You should be able to eliminate work as you narrow in on the problem. Good problem statements are immediately useful in helping you focus and make priority calls.

Remember, this work isn't easy. Getting to a strong Convergent Problem Statement is an iterative process. You'll need to be patient with yourself and expect to rewrite several problem statements multiple times before you narrow down and select. We encourage writing lots of rough drafts, sharing them, getting feedback, and going back to the drawing board (which may mean doing more customer research). Get feedback from people outside your product team—individuals who are not as close to the customer or the customer's problem will ask good questions, so use those individuals wisely!

The Convergent Problem Statement is just as useful for new products as it is to prioritize features for existing products. We love starting ideation with a couple of the most compelling problem statements, helping us to explore and ultimately prioritize which customer problem our business is best positioned to address. For product leaders—the best way to support your team is to be deeply involved and invested at this early stage. When you help your product manager (PM) work towards a Convergent Problem Statement, you set the Groundwork for a successful product. Here are some strategies to working with your PMs:

- **Insist that every "idea" be framed as a problem statement.** In our work, we've even created mini templates and asked anyone in the company to share product ideas, as long as they write the ideas in the form of a problem, and not a solution. This helps cut down the noise of new product ideas since there is the small hurdle of entering it as a well-formed problem statement. This is a great source of new ideas, and highlights people in the organization who are passionate about solving customer problems.
- **Share the iterations that helped you converge to the chosen problem.** You want to show by example that no one gets it right the first time. By showcasing examples, you provide a roadmap for how you want your product team to think. Many problem statements start with a lot of guesses, and then you refine them through learning. Show that journey for your teams to emulate.

- **Highlight "failures" or problem statements that ended up abandoned because you proved there wasn't actually a problem!** We've all been captivated by new product ideas, or solutions that we thought were so obvious, and when we do the work we uncover that customers had a simple workaround, or felt lukewarm toward the idea, or discovered the problem wasn't important enough to want to pay for a solution. We've shared when a customer's "good-enough" solution was sufficient or the pain wasn't high enough for them to choose an alternative. By highlighting examples, you demonstrate the rigor that brings a product or feature onto the roadmap. You'll see all the teams you work with gain confidence knowing that customers are waiting for their solution.

- **Never assign development resources unless you are satisfied that there is a genuine Convergent Problem Statement.** This can feel painful when there are engineers available and both you and your product manager feel the urgency to create work. You have to stay strong! You'll avoid much pain and suffering (also known as bad customer reviews, rework, and unhappy teams).

GROUNDWORK IN ACTION: XERO

Xero is a New Zealand-based company that offers cloud-based accounting software for small and medium-sized businesses. We wanted to share this story for several reasons; as former executives at Intuit, we used to watch Xero and it was fascinating getting the inside story. And, as one of Groundwork's authors is from New Zealand, it's with some personal pride that we get to showcase a company from that part of the world.

Andrew Tokeley (Tokes) was the first product manager for Xero's flagship online accounting product back in 2009. Over six years, he helped the product team grow from 20 people in a single office to over 400 in six offices across four countries. Tokes described the situation he was working in back in 2009 to us—how no one was talking about product management; it was all about agile practices and getting better at delivering software. There were no formally trained product managers, which makes his focus on watching customers and identifying clear problems to solve, even more impressive. Tokes ascribes the success of Xero to absolute alignment across the company on what was important to their customers. It was clear in our conversation that they identified very specific problems to solve and followed up with innovative solutions that changed how the market viewed financial accounting (and even changing how the national tax authority thought about data!).

We loved how Tokes recounted the tenacity by which he drove his team to understand the underlying challenges faced by his customers. Rather than framing the problem as simply enabling customers to achieve an accounting function, like invoicing, or any number of other accounting features, they kept asking themselves fundamental questions about why a feature was needed. For example, users send invoices to get paid, to remind their customers of payment terms and as an official record of work completed. They are documents shared with their clients, so they care how they look. Understanding what was important to the customer in these workflows led Tokes and his teams to create innovative solutions that went well beyond the somewhat dry accounting features to deliver delight.

Problem definition and discovery also involved watching customers, talking to them and learning how they thought about finances. This wasn't always easy and it sometimes meant making hard choices between different types of customers. For example, both accountants and their small business clients used Xero, and both needed to be understood and consulted with. The Xero team chose to change technical terms to more user-friendly language, leveraging the typical way that customers talked about their work. Tokes refers to this as the humanization of an inherently technical product. It was through this regular interaction with their users, that they built up significant trust and mutual respect that Tokes remains proud of to this day.

As a startup in an established industry in 2009, Xero stayed true to solving difficult problems. Their technical solution, cloud-based accounting software, was novel at the time, though now it seems like such an obvious solution. They remained close to their customers, focusing on real problems and changed the face of financial accounting as a result.

SUMMARY

We'd like to think by now you're completely convinced that starting with a Convergent Problem Statement is a critical part of your work deliverables and you're going to have everyone on your team start working on this immediately. We recommend creating one *readable* sentence derived from the template that every single person on the product team can share. Use that as the north star for your product, and refer to it often. Once you have this, and you start using it in every presentation and meeting you have, amazing things start to happen. Everyone working with you understands the purpose of your product, they ask great questions, and they challenge you in productive ways. Basically, your life as a product manager just becomes a whole lot easier.

■ ■ ■

3

GROUNDWORK PILLAR II: ACTIONABLE PERSONA

OKAY, YOU'VE just read about defining the problem in a way that converges your thinking and sets you on a focused path. Now we're going to talk about who you are solving that problem for, and how you define that "who" in an actionable way. In other words, we're going to talk about a persona.

Before diving into our definition of persona, let's start with how people commonly think of a persona. Alan Cooper, the founder of Alan Cooper Design and author of *The Inmates Are Running the Asylum* (Pearson, 2004), pioneered the use of personas in the 1980s as a practical design tool for high-tech products. In short, he defined personas as "hypothetical archetypes of actual users. Although they are imaginary, they are defined with significant rigor and precision."

Personas sprung from Alan's process of play-acting as users, hand gestures and all, while mentally walking through complex design decisions. By actually sitting in the shoes of one of his customers, he was able to see what was necessary and how to prioritize tasks within an experience. He embodied someone he deemed representative of his target user. While bystanders watching Alan in action might think him odd, his role-playing enabled him to make tough design tradeoffs quickly and effectively. This was Alan's "go-to" process that led to many successes. One of his little Broadway shows ended up serving as the model for what eventually became Microsoft® Project.

Alan wanted to package and communicate his play-acting practice into something his clients could understand and emulate in their own design initiatives. He began presenting proposed designs from the point of view of different user segments, that he called personas, and helped teams sit in the shoes of important groups of users and make targeted decisions. His clients saw, firsthand, the value in viewing designs through the lens of representative personas.

Over 30 years later, we still use personas. But as with any long-used artifact, the concept of a persona evolved and developed a reputation. In this case, personas have gotten a bad rap. We often get eye rolls when we broach this topic in our product training and coaching programs. "We already have personas and we don't use them" is the usual reaction. Our flippant response: You're not doing it right!

We jest, but Alan says it well: "The most powerful tools are always simple in concept, but they often must be applied with some sophistication." So, before you skip this chapter of the book because you "already have personas," stay open to the possibility that nuances in how they're implemented matter. We're going to shatter common beliefs and practices so that you establish a new, more actionable way of defining your customer persona and using that persona in each stage of your product development.

Here's how we define a Persona:

A living archetype of your primary target customer representing similar behaviors and characteristics among a group of individuals, actively used in day-to-day product decisions.

This definition allows you to have an effective customer artifact and avoid misuse of personas that are not clearly communicated or are oversimplified to one profile trait. Keep in mind that personas are directly tied to the problem you are solving. For every problem, there is a person you are solving that problem for and there is a unique set of needs that stem from that combination (person and problem), which we'll talk about in the next Pillar of Groundwork called *Individualized Needs*. When you are working on the Convergent Problem Statement, you must always keep in mind *who* you are solving the problem for through the definition of your persona.

WHAT A PERSONA IS NOT

We once walked into our client's building (name not mentioned to protect the innocent) and as part of the kickoff for the project, we asked for any documentation they had on their target customer. "You mean personas?" Yes! Exactly! They tapped out a message on Slack and minutes later, the UX designer walked into the conference room and placed three laminated, full color, 20" X 30" flip charts on the table. Each had four pages of detail, including pictures and text. Our eyes widened for just a second. As we started to thumb through the beautifully produced flip charts, we started asking questions.

- **How are these used?** We use them when we design or redesign areas of the UX.
- **Does the extended development team have copies of these?** No. They don't need them.
- **When was the last time you used them?** About three months ago, when we redesigned the onboarding experience.
- **How were these developed?** We hired a design firm to research and produce these for us.
- **How much did these personas cost?** We muttered that question to ourselves; we could make a ballpark guess given the production quality. Let's just say it was over $20,000.

They had big, beautiful, professionally created personas they could hang on the wall, and could even spill food and water on without issue! And the research team used them. So, what's the problem here? There were a few things:

It's Not a Contest to Write the Longest, Most Detailed Persona

Don't be fooled. Less is more here. You want the entire organization to know the personas, use them, and refer to them in all aspects of product planning and creation process. They need to be simple, easily communicated, and constantly referenced.

It's Not a Broad Persona

Too often we see wide swaths of the population depicted as the target market because they all experience the problem we're solving. Hence, we create a broadly scoped persona. That may include solving it for someone who has the problem but doesn't feel enough pain to act on that problem. This is a huge pitfall to avoid. Your target personas are only those willing to take the action you want them to in exchange for solving their problem; be it open their wallet, donate their time, respond to your communication, and so on.

One question we recommend asking during persona-related research is "What would you be willing to pay to have this problem solved?" or "What would it take for you to open your wallet to pay for this solution concept we're showing you?" or "What would you expect to pay for a solution like this?" Choose your own words to help you understand whether or not the research participant would be willing to take the action you want them to take. This is not meant to be a pricing discussion. We don't recommend interviews for pricing research. To be clear, you should be focusing on people who have expressed a willingness to pay, donate, or act to have their problem solved and not those that show a mere interest in solving the problem. Your persona will become clearer as you understand who is willing to pay and who isn't.

Note for B2B leaders: This point is relevant only to your buyer persona. It's much less relevant to users who aren't decision-makers. Keep that in mind as you interview and identify target personas. Though, you still want to understand the likelihood to use among those non-decision-makers, so your questions should include that for those profile and persona interviews.

It's Not About Outsourcing

Taking ownership of your customer is your job. Sorry. This is the Groundwork you and your team must do with your own hands. Interacting with customers, discussing what you learned with the team, and coming to a shared vision on your target persona is a requirement for creating products that customers love. Don't get us wrong—we do outsource research, but there is a time and place for outsourcing. For this aspect of the Groundwork, you need to learn from your customers firsthand.

It's Not A Laundry List of Demographics

Our client didn't make this mistake—they did a great job of deeply understanding the archetype and bringing each of these personas to life. But we frequently see personas represented as a list of demographics and a couple of attitudes, rendering the personas one dimensional and not actionable. Demographics are good for marketing, in terms of buying direct mail lists, filtering within social media campaigns, and calculating available market sizes. But bad for making product, and design decisions. You need to understand attitudes, behaviors, goals, a day-in-the-life, and similar information.

It Isn't A Job Description

Many B2B personas we see describe a job and the daily tasks within that job. A list of job responsibilities is very helpful when you're trying to understand where your problem space fits into the world of that persona and when you're identifying relevant needs (needs will be discussed in much more detail in Groundwork Pillar III) that must be addressed to solve the problem well. However, just knowing a person's daily job tasks tells you nothing about *who* the person is or *how* you should build an experience that delights them. So, in other words, a job description is helpful in describing the "what" you're going to do, but it doesn't give you any guidance on "how" you're going to do it. There are many ways to design a feature depending on the traits of your user. The feature addresses the task at hand but the design approach (the aesthetic, placement of buttons, vernacular used, types and number of steps to complete the task, etc.) will vary widely depending on *who* you are building that feature for. Avoid just focusing on what could turn into features (job tasks and responsibilities) and focus more on the inputs to your design approach (this person's aspirations and how they go about their daily life).

It Isn't "One-And-Done"

Personas are always evolving. Most of the time, you start with hypotheses about who your target user is. You're never right the first time. For example, you may assume your persona is focused on accuracy given that they are an accountant and spend a lot of time playing the role of "accuracy police" with their staff. But as you conduct more research to investigate their needs you find that, yes, accuracy is important, but they actually view themselves as a coach that helps their staff build good data hygiene. Think about how different you might design an accounting software experience for someone that views themselves as a coach to help others with their accuracy checking instead of someone that views themselves as the "accuracy police." The former might have the product team prioritizing data reconciliation functionality for the staff roles, while the latter might prioritize the ability to check their staff's work. It doesn't mean you can't do both, but it certainly would dictate your prioritization of the two areas of functionality.

As you conduct more research you will learn more about your target customer, proving or disproving your hypotheses and refining the persona. Without this refinement, personas get shelved and become out of touch with reality. If you spend thousands of dollars on beautifully produced and laminated artifacts, you're not going to want to change them, which means those artifacts eventually go out of date and won't be useful to anyone. Keep your personas fresh by taking time after every research study, big or small, and step back to ask yourself, "Does what we learned in this study change the way we think about our persona?" or "Does it change the assumptions we've made?" If either question is answered with a YES!, it is at this point that you will update your persona and communicate that to the broader development team with any implications that might have on efforts in the backlog or roadmap.

By the way, when it's a new product, this kind of refinement will happen more frequently. We've had periods, early on with a new product, where every study (discovery, concept test, usability, etc.) will result in some refinement to the persona and that's okay. It's even great, because you are getting closer to the core of your persona which will enable more confident and efficient decisions. As you enter later product lifecycle phases, that refinement will become less frequent if you've done the refinement earlier. You may also discover new personas to expand your market share.

Always think about your persona definition after every bit of research and pressure test the definition against new learning and refine it as you move forward.

WHY AN ACTIONABLE PERSONA IS SO IMPORTANT

A common misperception is that designing an experience for the broadest set of users with the broadest set of functionalities will drive the highest probability of business success. Too often we see product teams say "Our product serves many segments of the market," and the teams are unable to make decisions either because they're solving for too many personas, or their product is bloated with lots of bells and whistles, but doesn't quite meet the needs of any one segment well.

A 2006 Harvard Business Review (HBR) article said it well: "Design products that do one thing very well... Too often, in their eagerness to layer on additional functionality, developers lose sight of the product's basic function—the one thing it must do extremely well."[9] That sounds a bit too simplistic and impractical, but let's examine a simple example:

A Simple Example

Imagine that you're building an electric drill. (Yes, we're talking about drills again!) There are at least three clear segments (and personas) that need a drill: a professional contractor (George), a woman DIYer (Patty), and a woodworking artist (Terry). There are many product attributes to consider in the design: handle size and shape, drill bit variability for

---

[9] "Defeating Feature Fatigue." Harvard Business Review, February 2006; Rolan T. Rust, Debora Viana Thompson, and Rebecca Hamilton.

surface and size, button size and location, cord length, power options, motor strength, etc.

Let's get to know our personas a bit more:

- **George (professional contractor)** is trying to build a structure out of wood with varying density, to regulatory code, and on a deadline. He uses his tools 5 to 8 hours a day in dirty, hot, and sometimes wet environments.
- **Patty (DIYer)** is hanging pictures on drywall and putting furniture together. She does these tasks once every few months, at most, and always inside the walls of her or her parents' home.
- **Terry (woodworking artist)** works out of his garage with Snakewood and Barauna, two of the hardest, most dense types of wood in the world, building high-end furniture and custom decorative pieces. He requires precision and minimum impact of his building tools on the final design as his furniture is considered art.

Imagine if you had to build a drill for all three of these individuals and maybe more! For Terry, the drill motor would have to penetrate hardwood with precision and the drill bits would need to ensure minimal scarring around the hole. This means a bigger motor, making the drill more expensive than necessary for, say, Patty. To serve all three people you'd have to include many drill bits to accommodate multiple uses and materials.

And how do you build a drill to best fit Patty's hand *and* George's? On average the hand length of a woman is about 1.2 inches smaller than that of a man. Do you build adjustable or replaceable handles in multiple sizes? What would that do to the overall integrity of the drill if it were used on a construction site? The casing would have to be heavy-duty to withstand the elements at George's construction site, but how does that impact the size and weight of the drill for Patty, or its ability to accommodate odd angles around furniture for Terry?

And do you make this cordless with a 5-to-8-hour battery life for George without pricing either Terry or Patty out? Or do you build it with a shorter battery life (lower cost and weight) and force George to use multiple batteries each day? Have we beaten this dead horse enough yet? The prioritization and tradeoff decisions are numerous and trying to solve for the needs of George, Patty, *and* Terry dilutes the utility or value for any one of them, not to mention how much deliberation, and delay, is necessary to make any specific tradeoff.

By the way, could we make this drill completely configurable? Sure! For a cost. This is an approach that many companies take to ensure they cover as much of the market as possible. In the late 1990s and early 2000s, Mercedes-Benz introduced hundreds of features in their cars. They were attempting to solve for every possible need across many segments of the population. They later realized that the vast majority of features they'd added to their cars were not being used at all because they were either unknown to customers or too complex to use. Mercedes-Benz had made the overall customer experience frustrating, rather than creating the luxurious experience they were aiming for. And it cost them a lot of money to test and maintain all the new features. They eventually removed 600—yes, 600—features from their cars, and simplified the most important features and creature comforts in their cars.

Spending money and time on all those bells and whistles only to have to remove them is not an easy or cheap task! But developing personas, if done right, could have helped Mercedes-Benz in preventing a situation like this. Knowing who they were solving for, their attitudes, their driving behaviors, their tech aptitude, etc., could have all helped in prioritizing investments in the experience. Personas done right offer huge value to an organization. Let's look at the benefits of personas.

Personas Enable Easy Design Decisions

Okay, this is probably the one for which you say *No duh!* but indulge us. Personas make your design decisions easy, yes, but not just because personas are documented. What's critical is bringing these people, channeled through personas, into your decision room (metaphorically speaking), and asking the following questions to simplify your design decisions:

- Would George (one of our personas from the drill example) understand how to use this if we built it this way?

- How would George translate this?
- What would George do next?

Let's say that George is your primary persona and Terry and Patty were secondary. Your team could confidently decide what to focus on in the drill design because you know who is most important and what they need. You'd also be clear about the implications your design decisions have for the other two personas. It doesn't mean you can't decide to strike a balance between George and Terry's needs for a particular feature, but that would be a conscious choice, and not a haphazard debate about features and prioritization of design elements.

Personas Enable Efficient, Effective, and Durable Decisions

Having an agreed-upon persona also forces the decision-making process out of the opinion space and into predetermined criteria that people can get behind. Many people come to the table with different views of who they are solving a problem for and most of the time they don't realize the decision is going off track until it gets delayed unnecessarily or overturned altogether. Bringing a clear definition of the persona(s) as a foundation for a decision discussion ensures differences of opinion are exposed early and cleared up quickly. This way, when the team makes a decision it stays made.

Product leaders and product managers, more so than any other role in an organization, are expected to drive decisions across multiple business functions that don't directly report to them. This ability to drive decisions across teams is a skill that must be mastered to effectively do the job. Making decisions that are data-based, customer-backed, and criteria-driven will help you master this skill. And the problem statement and persona are artifacts to be used in every product decision, big or small.

In your next meeting when someone introduces a product idea, we challenge you to ask two questions and have each person write their answer down on a piece of paper: *Who are we solving for? What are we solving?* Then have each person share their response with the group. See if you get the same answers around the table. Chances are you won't, and you'll debate this product idea without really agreeing on what or who you are solving for, probably delaying any sort of decision.

Personas Give You Permission to Say "No"

Let's face it, as product leaders you are getting "great ideas" from everywhere, and in many cases, it's almost impossible to say no to any of them. These shiny objects end up in a backlog with the important roadmap initiatives and other justified priorities. Knowing who you're solving for, and therefore who you're not solving for, allows you to make design tradeoffs with justification and confidence. Referring back to George, Patty, and Terry and their needs for a hand drill, if you knew which of these personas was your priority, it would be easy to make decisions like drill shape and handle size, power requirements, etc. It would also help you understand what you can say no to. For instance, if you're prioritizing Patty, you can probably deprioritize making the drill casing waterproof for now.

Your persona, if actionable by incorporating the items mentioned in "Elements of An Actionable Persona" and acknowledged by the organization, is your permission to say no with clear justification to shiny objects.

ELEMENTS OF AN ACTIONABLE PERSONA

What does an Actionable Persona look like? We already talked about why a persona is important and the fact that all of the Groundwork ensures the best possible experience at the lowest possible cost, but let's get deeper into what it looks like to have an effective persona in your product creation process. We're going to share a Persona Template we incorporate into all our training.

We say a persona is effective when you can easily take action against it, like making a product decision. An effective persona is actionable. It's incorporated into all aspects of the product creation process. Whether it's building strategy, defining a roadmap, making design decisions, or making backlog tradeoffs. It's about actively referencing this persona in discussions with your product team.

Here is a real example using our Persona Template to develop a persona for a mobile fitness application. Meet Melanie, an actual persona we used in our business.

MELANIE

"Let's Do It!"

Summary Background

Melanie values an active lifestyle over most other things in her life. She is focused on work/life balance and doesn't think of exercise as "working out" or optional. If she doesn't stay active, she feels tired and less productive in everything she does in her life. She's just not herself.

Goal: To minimize boredom while staying active; ultimately maintaining high energy and mental clarity in every day life

Relevant Behaviors

- Works out 4+ times per week
- Consistently active with an inconsistent set of activities
- Has 1-2 activities she does every week (gym, swim, yoga, etc.) but then mixes it up the rest of the week...hiking, running, SUP, etc.
- Has been or is a member of a studio or gym
- Doesn't own a PC, her mobile phone and iPad is all she needs

Relevant Attitudes

- *"I'll prioritize spending on fitness activities over other things."*
- *"I won't be cooped up in a gym all the time. I need to be outdoors."*
- *"My social life revolves around my active lifestyle. I choose friends who are as active as I am."*
- *"Don't make me read instructions, just let me do it!"*
- *"Life is about balance."*

Other/Relevant Demographics

- 25-40 Years old
- Employed full time
- $50K+ income
- Fitness spend per month $50+

The Melanie persona encompasses the *whole* person. A well-formed persona brings a real person to life even if it's an archetype of a group of people. There are several aspects of a person we recommend investigating to formulate your persona.

Summary Background

This is where we characterize a day-in-the-life of this person. What gets them up in the morning? What are they proud of? What is their work ethic? Include whatever paints a picture of who this person is.

Goals

This should be right out of your problem statement. It's what the person wants to achieve.

Relevant Behaviors

These are the behaviors in and around the problem space, and also behaviors that inform your solution. For example, Melanie's mobile devices are her PC, so to speak. So, we started with a mobile-first strategy until we expanded into other personas.

Relevant Attitudes

These are not only attitudes about the problem at hand, but also attitudes that inform how you design your experience. Melanie's attitude of "Don't make me read instructions, just let me do it!" isn't necessarily relevant in fitness, but it's very relevant to how we think about the level of handholding and instruction we'd provide in the product.

Relevant Demographics

We talked about this earlier in this chapter. We list these last because they are the last thing to worry about. A few demographics might be helpful in particular situations. For instance, knowing Melanie's income was important when we thought about an appropriate price range for the value proposition. And knowing she had a 9-to-5 job helps guide our strategy for fitness schedules, which focused on studios and classes that fit around the schedule of someone with a full-time job, versus a stay-at-home mom, for instance. So, demographics can be helpful, but are less critical than other factors. As you'll see in the Groundwork Pillar III: Individualized Needs chapter, the combination of needs and persona trivializes a bunch of demographics.

All that being said, we recommend using a single set of personas across the company so you're all talking to the same people and therefore presenting a single front to your customers. As such, demographics are important to your marketing folks, so you probably won't avoid them altogether.

Character Trait Spectrums (for Design)

Think about the spectrums of character traits that matter. We often talk about this concept as trait spectrums. These are spectrums of character traits that aid in design decisions, like technical aptitude, confidence in trying new things, level of patience in learning new things, and social media behavior. There are a multitude of trait spectrums that are highly valuable within different customer experience mediums (software, hardware, brick-and-mortar, etc.). Here is a list that we use as a starting point:

- Visionary … Pragmatic?
- Organized … Disorganized?
- Controlling … Delegates?
- Analytical … Free-thinking?
- Tech-savvy … Tech-phobic?
- Quick Learner … Slow learner?
- Patient … Impatient?
- Over Communicative … Isolationist?
- Rebel … Rule follower?
- Confident … Not confident?

You can see how each of these might change your approach to your overall value proposition, including the workflow, the vernacular in or around the experience, and how you market it. Knowing where your persona lands on some of these spectrums (or others) is invaluable to creating an experience that delights your customers. What are some trait spectrums that pertain to your product or service and the environment or medium through which it is experienced?

Firmographics, Business Vertical

One thing you didn't see in the persona above, because it was a B2C example, is the idea of firmographics and business verticals. For B2B, this matters a lot. A person who works for a small business has a very different job and set of responsibilities than a person in a Fortune 500 company. Even if two people have the same title, the environments within which they work differ, their pressures differ, their actual job tasks are probably at very different scales, and their lifestyles may also differ.

The vertical can also be important in certain circumstances. For instance, QuickBooks is a small business financial management software product. Of the companies that use it, inventory-based businesses have significantly different challenges than service-based businesses. And within inventory-based businesses, a medical supply company had different regulatory and reporting constraints than a hobby shop. These differences needed to be called out in our persona to ensure we were designing for the challenges of the particular vertical.

Willingness to Act

We talked about this briefly earlier in the chapter. Your personas should represent people who are willing to act in return for having their problem solved. "Act" could mean pay, donate, or any number of other actions. A persona shouldn't be a broad segment of users that merely experience the same problem. It's deeper than that. As you do your research, make sure you ask questions that help you distinguish between someone willing to pay (or act), from someone that won't.

Research-Based

We always start with what we know *and* any hypotheses about our persona. Then we develop a research plan to prove or disprove those hypotheses and evolve from there. The point is that personas should be based on actual quantitative and qualitative data. The data doesn't always have to come from statistically valid sample sizes, as you will read in the Practices chapters, but it does need to be based on real customer interaction.

Written In their Voice

You want the persona to feel like a real person. The more real the persona is, the more memorable it is for the rest of the team and the more actionable it becomes. Let's look at a scenario from a company building a SaaS application targeted at large cloud-based IT operations. We asked them to put together a persona for one of their critical users: the person in charge of cloud operations; called CloudOps. This person makes sure the lights are on for the rest of the organization, digitally speaking. Here is one behavior listed on the company's first version of the persona for the CloudOps manager:

The Relevant Behavior: "He is the gatekeeper to data and analytics platforms that the company is adopting."

This is merely a statement, and it's not written in the user's voice. It doesn't necessarily tell the product team who this person is. Instead, the statement describes how the author of the persona views the persona's job. It also doesn't lend itself to any decisions about design approach or anything else.

Now let's draft up a couple of alternatives, using what we've learned so far and written in the user's voice:

- Alternative 1: "I create hurdles for my company's users who log in to certain apps so they won't hurt themselves or the company."
- Alternative 2: "I make the platform open to solve my team's needs, as long as they know the risks."

Both of these alternatives could still represent the "gatekeeper" persona that the original relevant behavior wording referred to. However, Alternative 1 represents someone who sees themselves almost like a cop or a controller. You might prioritize features that allow CloudOps to limit the employees' usage to ensure there are no unintended or intended security breaches. Alternative 2, while still evoking a gatekeeper persona, indicates a person who sees his fellow employees more as team members than kids needing protection; wanting to enable them to be successful by doing what they need to do as long as they handle the risks responsibly. Here, you might prioritize features like in-app messaging or a content system that enables CloudOps to communicate specific risks or instructions that help the team make more informed decisions on the platform.

Alternative 1 and 2 describe different people. To delight the person that needs to have ultimate control versus the person that needs to enable informed freedom, you might choose to use different language within the product, design the information architecture differently, or prioritize tasks differently. Either of the alternatives make your persona much more actionable than the original relevant behavior statement.

Your goal is to bring the persona to life by standing in their shoes and expressing their beliefs, attitudes, and behaviors through their voice. This ensures a highly actionable persona for the entire team to use.

While this is a software-centric example, it demonstrates how bringing an attitude or behavior to life through the customer's voice makes a big difference in what you would build or offer, be that a tangible product or a service experience.

The Perfect Photo

Research shows that we remember things more vividly and retain them longer when we associate meaning to them using semantic encoding[10]. That means that the more deeply we process information, for example, by attaching meaning, emotion, or related knowledge to sensory input (e.g., visual, tactile, etc.), the stronger our memories are.

The sensory input in our persona is the photo. We spend a lot of time looking for the perfect photo that demonstrates the gestalt of a persona to ensure our extended team can easily recall who this person is and therefore, take action accordingly.

Check out Melanie in Figure 3-1 again. What do you see? She's on a mountain top. She's in her hiking gear with her backpack on the ground next to her. She's in the sun. She's got her thumb up and it appears much

---

[10] Craik, Fergus & Tulving, Endel. (1975). Depth of Processing and the Retention of Words in Episodic Memory. Journal of Experimental Psychology: General. 104. 268-294. 10.1037/0096-3445.104.3.268.

larger than everything else in the picture. She's smiling. Every aspect of this picture builds on the character of this persona. She's an active adventurer who is up for new outdoor experiences that promote her happiness.

Make sure you spend time finding the right photo. Too often we see personas with stock photography of a person sitting at their desk, posed for the camera. That won't help your team. Think about the person's mannerisms, facial expressions, clothing, and environment.

Team Buy-In

Your job is to infuse customer insights into the broader team's work, not just present the personas. It's about your ability to help the team get to know the persona as a person and to enable them to stand in the shoes of this person while doing their job. We've observed, through years of experience, that the deeper our extended team's understanding of the customer, the less we have to rehash requirements for the project and the less rework we see.

Back in the late 1990s, when both of us were at Intuit, Heather was on the QuickBooks team and Vidya was on the TurboTax team. We were just implementing the concept of Follow Me Home across the company. This was a form of ethnographic research where we conduct onsite observational research sessions. We'd go to our customer's place of work or place of filling out their taxes and quietly observe the process of managing finances or taxes.

The QuickBooks team conducted a bunch of these Follow Me Home sessions with small businesses and invited our engineers to observe. There was an interesting side effect of this. We found these engineers going home on a Friday after seeing and hearing these customers firsthand, and coming back on Monday having fixed an issue they observed in one of the sessions. They were so excited (and frustrated) by what they saw during the observational session that they couldn't help but try and make the users' experience better. We were seeing things like this across the company. The point is that seeing and hearing your target customer is by far more valuable than reading any documented persona.

There are a couple of things to consider in achieving this kind of intimacy and motivation:

- **Get your extended team participating in the research whenever possible.** Observing everything firsthand is far superior to waiting to get the CliffsNotes version. It's not always possible, but you'll get the best outcomes if the majority of your extended team has seen and heard your target users through observation or interaction. If they can't participate, then organize ways for them to view or listen to the recordings of your interactions. Brown bag lunch anyone?

- **Debrief the team on what you all learned through the research before putting pen to paper to write the persona.** Make them feel just as much ownership over the persona as you do. The more ownership they feel, the more they will utilize personas; ensuring consistency and delight in the user experience they are all working hard to develop.

- **Share what you learned first.** When you learn something new through research that leads to an evolution of the persona, make sure you share the learning before reposting a new version of the persona. Focus on the infusion of learning about the persona and the implication of that learning on what the team is working on. Focus on this more than on presentation of the persona.

Used in All Product Decisions

We talked about this briefly and we'll elaborate a bit more here. Whether you're deciding on strategy, building a roadmap, making a design decision, or trying to make a backlog tradeoff, your persona should always be sitting in that room with you. We mean this literally. Hang the persona (including the perfect photo) in the room where you make decisions. While you and your team stand in the shoes of that person, ask questions like the ones below:

- Does this solve [your persona's name]'s problem or address their top needs? Why or why not?
- Would [your persona's name] pay for this? Why or why not?
- What does [your person's name] need first?
- What would [your persona's name] do here?
- How would [your persona's name] translate this?

Discuss the answers with the team. Don't assume you all know the same information. Hear each team member's perspective and review data together if necessary. If you can't answer these questions in the meeting because you don't have the data, then form a hypothesis to use for now and do a scrappy test. (See the **Practice I: Developing Hypothesis Practice** and **II: Conducting Scrappy Research** chapters for more on this.)

You'll know you've mastered this discipline when your extended team starts asking, unprompted, "Who are we solving for?" or "How would [your persona's name here] react to this?"

Simplicity

We like the acronym K.I.S.S., though we like a softer version: Keep It Super Simple. We try to stick to one-page personas. It's not easy. If it were, we wouldn't be writing this book. Every statement on your persona should be additive and actionable. Let's talk about what we mean by these two terms:

- **Additive:** Do not repeat yourself even if you use different, prettier language. Each element of the persona should hold unique value that contributes to bringing the person to life. Duplication takes up precious space that could be used for an additional valuable characteristic of this person.
- **Actionable:** Make sure that every element is actionable. Make sure each element can be used in a product decision, be it strategy, road mapping, design, or backlog. If you don't know if an element is actionable, then pressure test it against a recent decision you struggled with or one that is coming up. If you still aren't sure, then keep as part of the persona and check back over time to make sure that all the elements are used at one time or another. Not all elements will be used for every decision, so don't make this harder than it is. Just be thoughtful about what you add to your persona.

Continually Validated/Evolved

You and your team are constantly learning from research, customer interactions, and actual engagement with your product or service. As such, the persona you are creating will evolve. Make a point to validate hypotheses you've made about the persona. Every time you interact with customers, whether during research or otherwise, check whether or not the persona definition has changed. The personas are only as valuable as the data they reflect. It's okay to update personas (or even identify subsegments that constitute different personas) that result in uncovering new problems and opportunities for the business. Periodic persona updates are healthy. We recommend doing a check every 6 months (less for newer products) if not after every major research effort. Don't let more than a year go by. At least refresh personas during the planning season.

Go back to the example of Melanie we started this chapter with and let's walk through a couple of thought exercises using this persona to demonstrate what it means to be actionable. As we stated, Melanie is an actual persona we used for a fitness application we developed.

◆ ◆ ◆

EXERCISE 1

Using Personas in Developing Product Strategy

In our company's early stages, we had a lot of input from investors, our board, and other leaders in the organization as to what product strategy we should take early on with the fitness app we were developing. Here are the paths we were considering given what we knew at the time and the inputs we were getting from all of these stakeholders.

Strategic Path #1: Achieve Goals with Others

Features included:

- Social gaming infrastructure; leveraging activity, health metrics, and reputation rewards
- Goal setting and goal management
- Virtual coaching
- Group invites, competition, and tracking
- Social media integration

Strategic Path #2: Find and Stick with My Sweet Spot

Features included:

- Focus on quantity of most popular genres (yoga, spin, CrossFit) with classes around work hours
- Reserve multiple weeks of same class; set weekly schedules
- Reviews of instructors
- Studio-specific volume discounts
- Last-minute cancelation ability

Strategic Path #3: Discover New & Fun Stuff

Features included:

- Member profiling; gleaning adventure level, level of strenuousness
- "Discover Fun Exercise" algorithm and matching
- Reviews and ratings of fitness genres
- Focus on quantity and variety of genres
- Platform volume discounts

Which path do you think we chose? Strategic Path #1 was what our investors aimed for. Virtual coaching was a huge trend in the fitness app space, as was building virality in the user experience. Strategic Path #2 was what one of our team members, a fitness fanatic, wanted. She felt that we needed to solve for finding the best instructors and ensuring users would exercise more with finding the best instructor. That's what she found successful for her. Both of these were credible strategies, but the path we chose was Strategic Path #3. This best solved for Melanie and optimized our opportunity.

There were a few behaviors and attitudes within our Melanie persona that helped us reach this decision. The fact that she was "consistently active with an inconsistent set of activities" was a clue. We knew she got bored easily. That's how we knew our focus should be on discovery of new fitness genres. Additionally, Melanie already belonged to a studio and had her ritual activities set. She wasn't looking to find a new permanent studio. Nothing in her persona described her needing to attain a fitness goal. All of this added up to us putting a stake in the ground at Strategic Path #3 and moved forward.

This isn't to say we weren't going to expand and tackle other segments and strategies as we grew. But we used the persona to prioritize and move forward. We were able to confidently justify this direction and connect it back to who we were solving for. It gave our investors the confidence that we knew what we were doing and drove commitment across our company's leaders so we could move forward.

◆ ◆ ◆

EXERCISE 2

Using Personas in Deciding on an Approach to Feature Design

In working on the onboarding experience for our fitness application we thought about three different design approaches given some of the ideas the team had and what we had seen in other fitness apps.

Design Approach #1

- Drop Melanie into a step-by-step experience, with hand-holding at each step, offering in-line help, and a prompted chatbot to help her build confidence (and efficiency) in using the app.

Design Approach #2

- Melanie is dropped into an automated tour of the app with three on-screen feature description cues that can be skipped if desired.

Design Approach #3

- No onboarding experience. Melanie is dropped into her first fitness class search experience and is off and running.

After reviewing Melanie's persona again, which design approach is most appropriate? We hope you chose Design Approach #3. Melanie is a confident, active mobile user, and has no patience for learning how to do something before just doing it. This is stated clearly in her persona: "Don't make me read instructions, just let me do it!" As a team, we were able to make this decision, with confidence, very quickly and never look back.

We didn't waste any time on building out tours or step-by-step onboarding experiences. We didn't even spend time developing a lot of in-app help in our first version. Instead, we focused on simplicity and common mobile user interface standards to minimize the learning curve and get Melanie on her merry way immediately. It saved us a lot of money and minimized the time-to-value for her. Don't get us wrong, designing for simplicity isn't easy, but instead of focusing on help and onboarding tours we focused on making the experience drop dead simple.

Making this decision required us to know a lot about Melanie—more than just the traditional demographics or her goals. We needed to know her tech habits and her attitudes and approach to trying new things, including new technology. Our targeted and in-depth knowledge of Melanie was critical in making the right decisions early on, versus spending a lot of resources on technology we didn't need or on an experience that could have limited Melanie's onboarding experience altogether.

Both of these exercises required more than Melanie's age or profession to understand what she needed from the experience. So be sure to spend time on thoroughly understanding who the persona is; bring them to life.

◆ ◆ ◆

GROUNDWORK IN ACTION: KHAN ACADEMY

The Khan Academy is a highly innovative edtech company that serves millions of learners and has developed one of the most effective online global platforms for personalized learning. It has made huge strides in making learning engaging for students and proving its efficacy though higher academic test scores in grades K-12. It takes "learning at your own pace" to a whole new level.

Ginny Lee, President and COO of Khan Academy, shared a pivotal moment where the leadership team decided to move their focus away from a segment they called "independent learners"; a base of about 18 million (all ages and many different learning goals) and decided to focus on the narrower base of in-classroom K-12 students, with even further focus on the underserved student as defined by African-American, Latinx, and low-income.

The concept of independent learners, while a large segment of the market, spanned multiple, significantly different subsegments, encompassing kindergarten through adult learning; in and out of school. The team was making user experience decisions that tried to serve all students and struggled to see the important results that donors and funding sources needed to see; namely metrics that normally would be associated with course completion. And although a learner base of about 18 million coming to their site each month sounded like a resounding success, they learned some very interesting things.

The primary thing they learned was the majority of learners were curious people, proactively coming to learn, but never really finishing a course, nor was there an accredited baseline to measure growth or proficiency gains in learning. Their curiosity ran dry and life went on. So, while donors were enamored by the 18 million sets of eyeballs, they weren't seeing the outcomes expected, like improved standardized test scores for young learners or career advancement measures for adult learners. Those outcomes that normally come with completion of courses.

Focusing on the broad spectrum of independent learners, without a clear persona, it was difficult to decide what to do next. Which problem do you solve? A couple examples:

- Focusing on adult learners looking to learn to code in a particular programming language to make themselves more marketable might lead you to focus on building tangible certificates learners could present to hiring managers. Or to formulate the instructional and learning materials to coincide with roles at companies hiring programmers with various skill levels (e.g., level 1 programmer, level 2 programmer).

- In contrast, focusing on the classroom grade-schooler in a geographic area with lower than average graduation rates, you might create an experience for the teacher to assign additional practice questions, tools to help with differentiated learning, and dashboards to monitor and support students' progress with the academic curriculum.

Khan Academy realized that defining a persona was the answer to deciding what to do next. They chose the in-classroom K-12 student as their target customer. That decision helped the team focus their time observing classroom learning and gaining deep knowledge about the classroom, the K-12 learning experience, the relevant learning-related needs within the classroom context, and the impactful relationships involved in student success. In addition, the team conducted observational sessions with the parents of these students, teachers, and the district administration team. Khan Academy's persona decision allowed them to focus their research and make targeted user experience decisions, which drove increased-engagement for the K-12 student learning experience and statistically significant improvements in standardized test scores.

As a result of these improvements in engagement and test scores, Khan Academy partnered with Northwest Evaluation Association (NWEA), a non-profit organization that provides nationally recognized, research-based adaptive assessments, professional development, and research services in the U.S., extending Khan Academy's reach deeper into the classroom across hundreds of thousands of additional students. With this strategic partnership, students would take an in-class interim assessment administered by NWEA so teachers know where each student stands. Then every student automatically gets placed on a personalized learning pathway on Khan Academy where the students practice on differentiated instruction with high-quality content. And with that closed feedback loop from the accredited NWEA assessment to practice on Khan Academy, students and teachers can gain insights to better personalize the instruction and quantitatively measure the impact and growth in learning proficiency. The single decision to refocus on a specific, richly defined persona changed the trajectory of their growth and efficacy, globally.

GROUNDWORK IN ACTION: 99DESIGNS

One of the sectors that most commonly objects to using personas is clients in the B2B and marketplace spaces. They tell us that their companies are too complex, that they serve too many different types of people—from users, to clients, to decision makers—and they can't possibly use a small number of personas to make key decisions. Our go-to example of working at TurboTax, with over 20 million customers, was demonstrating that we were using about seven personas (a product to serve each one uniquely) doesn't seem to convince them. In fact, it only serves to strengthen their argument that we are describing a B2C environment, and that we can't possibly understand the complexity. So, we thought we'd turn to a company with a massively diverse marketplace to find out how they leverage personas and how they learn from them.

Established in 2008, 99designs is a platform that connects designers to businesses and has helped over 500,000 businesses worldwide develop creative content; logos, website design, and such. We even hired a 99designs artist for our Product Rebels logo. 99designs started with a group of designers who were competing to create the best digital designs. This friendly competition transformed into a unique design marketplace that now helps designers all over the world by matching them with every different type of client, from individuals to small businesses, to big companies.

Ashish Desai, former Chief Product Officer at 99designs[11], was hired as their first product manager back in 2012. We wanted to know what the company thought about personas, and if they used them in their marketplace environment which has so many different types of interactions. Turns out they use between 10 to 15 personas on a regular basis. They keep these personas relevant and meaningful through an ongoing expectation that their product people are always curious and learning about their customers. Ashish tells us they learned to create

---

[11] Ashish was Chief Product Officer at the time of our discussion. He left 99designs in July 2019, to lead Product at Handshake.

their own personas after a hard lesson. The product team brought in an external consultant to create a set of personas. The results were cute, catchy, and easy to remember. We see this a lot when teams outsource persona development to professional designers or marketers. Once you've paid for artifacts that look that good (and cost a lot), you want to use them.

The catchy personas led 99designs to overdesign the user experience for these personas that were, in essence, shallow stereotypes. They wasted way too much time solving for customers that they, as a team, didn't really understand. They made key decisions based on these externally developed personas without investing time to get to know their own customers. The result was that they over-solved for particular customers and missed some critical customer segments completely. They learned from that lesson, and now the company expects their product managers to learn about and understand customers directly. Ashish modeled this behavior by calling customers regularly (especially those who left negative feedback through one of their feedback channels). 99designs developed core persona's themselves and constantly update them based on what they learn from continuously talking with customers.

Ashish built in a requirement that everyone on his team must understand the user. Whether by participating in user Slack channels, reviewing their Net Promoter Score (NPS) open-ended survey responses, calling users who provided negative feedback, listening in on support calls, or reviewing open-ended feedback provided through each transaction. Ashish expects everyone in the company, not just the product team, to maintain some connection with users daily. The company attributes much of their customer delight and growth to the ongoing practice of customer learning and to having a crystal-clear understanding of who they are solving for.

SUMMARY

Let's Recap:

- The Persona, just like the Problem Statement, is a critical piece of the Groundwork required to drive focus, enable fast and effective decisions, and ensure the most targeted and delightful user experience possible. The Problem Statement and Persona combination, essentially the *what* and the *who*, always go hand in hand in every decision you make, big and small.

■ Our definition of a Persona: *A living archetype of your primary target customer representing similar behaviors and characteristics among a group of individuals, actively used in day-to-day product decisions.*

■ A successful persona has the following properties:
  ◆ It encompasses the whole person
  ◆ It's research-based
  ◆ It's written in the customer's voice
  ◆ It has the perfect photo
  ◆ It has team buy-in
  ◆ It's used in all product decisions
  ◆ It's simple and one-page long
  ◆ It's evolving as you learn

■ ■ ■

4

GROUNDWORK PILLAR III: INDIVIDUALIZED NEEDS

If I had asked my customers what they wanted, they would have said a faster horse.

THIS IS a great quote by Henry Ford. Imagine if folks only produced what people said they wanted. We may never have experienced air travel. We never asked for the smartphone, but could you see your life without one now?

Let's start with defining a need before defining what we mean by individualized. In this section we talk about the customer's needs relative to the problem you are solving and who you're solving it for. Every problem-persona combination has a unique set of needs that, if effectively prioritized, will round out your Groundwork and strengthen focus and successful innovation, resulting in the ultimate customer delight. We call the list of prioritized needs by problem-persona combination individualized needs.

Needs are often bypassed because product managers jump straight from observations to solutions or features. They don't pause to understand what is behind or surrounding the problems they observe through research. We'll go so far as to say customer research without translation into needs is useless. We must do the work to make sense of the data in front of us. Here's how we define Needs:

Aspects of the problem, for a particular persona, that your solution must address.

Needs can be latent or overt. Overt needs are obvious; they're usually mentioned by your customer or they're obvious when you observe them in their day-to-day tasks or jobs. A need may reveal itself when you listen to a customer complain that your product doesn't work for them. Customers often state what's missing or why your product is insufficient or defective. Translation of a complaint into a need is usually pretty straightforward. However, latent needs require more work. Latent needs are hidden from plain sight. Oftentimes people don't realize they have a need and you can only identify those needs through observation and deeper root-cause questions about their problem.

IDENTIFY NEEDS

So, don't just look for the obvious stuff. Pay attention to why someone does something and nuanced workarounds that can result in truly golden innovation. Here are some ways to identify needs:

Look for Task Inefficiencies

Do you see a highly inefficient or painful task associated with the problem you are solving for a persona? What makes it painful? How might you turn it into a valuable aspect of your eventual solution or experience?

For instance, as founders of a mobile fitness application that offered diverse fitness classes in a variety of genres through a single mobile experience, we learned that the persona (remember Melanie?) waited until the last minute to decide how she was going to get her exercise on any given day. She never knew exactly what time she'd get off work or how she'd feel after a long day's work. This pained her because she often couldn't reserve a spot in class at the last-minute. In turn, this minimized her fitness choices at the end of her day, which many times resulted in Melanie going home, without working out at all because she didn't feel like repeating a fitness activity she had done earlier that week. Melanie's unpredictable schedule and the consequences of last-minute planning were needs we had to address to successfully solve her overall problem: boredom and decreased motivation that comes with exercise repetition.

Check Environmental Context

Where does the problem you're solving take place? Are there environmental factors you should consider in your solution? Do environmental factors impact the frequency or level of pain experienced with the problem?

The list of environmental factors varies widely for each persona and could vary in prominence for each persona for which you are solving. For example, we knew that Melanie wouldn't travel more than 2 to 3 miles from home or work to exercise, regardless of the time of day or day of the week. We had to do more than just choose fitness genres that the persona would like. We had to focus on proximity as well. It proved to be one of the more challenging needs in our problem space.

Consider Baseline Market Expectations

Many times, there are baseline expectations for how adjacent, substitute, or competitive products work in your product space. Knowing those baseline expectations in your space, a.k.a. the costs of doing business, is critical as you think about solving a problem. Here are some examples:

- **Minimum switching costs.** What are the switching costs and how do they impact your solution scope? This may relate to where the majority of your prospects with the problem you are solving live. Or whether they use a competitor's product and will have to migrate data from one system to another. Do customers have to upend their long-term relationships with their current vendor? Are they using a substitute they created themselves, in which they have a significant amount of time, money, and training invested, but it's now antiquated? Do you have to scope a seamless transition? Why or why not?

- **Cultural norms.** How do prospects expect to interact with your solution or other adjacent or competitive solutions in the problem space? For example, how would social distancing impact user experience requirements if you were a golf cart manufacturer?

- **Industry-specific expectations.** What are some of the standards in the industry or solution medium that you have to meet (beyond regulatory)? For example, mobile UI standards have been set. We've grown accustomed to how to delete records, add items to a list, how search works, and so on. Most industries and experience mediums (e.g., mobile or web operating systems and applications, consumer electronics, retail, etc.) hold some standards and baseline expectations you should at least understand, rather than ignore them and build your own new interaction patterns. In some cases, it's cheaper for your team if standards exist because you don't need to reinvent the wheel. In other cases, adhering to the standards can be very costly or required if the standards today are suboptimal.

- **Substitute experience habits.** What are people currently familiar with that you must carry into a replacement experience? For example, when Intuit was developing Quicken back in the 1980s, the product team knew they were switching people from handwritten check registers that people were familiar and comfortable with, to digital records, and that the transition would be uncomfortable given the importance of financial management in a person's life. The team knew they needed to bring that familiarity into the digital experience. The check register in Quicken, although automated, looked like the check register customers were already comfortable with, which helped acclimate customers to what the application did for them. It helped ease their lack of comfort with moving their financial management to a whole new medium. It was a need Intuit couldn't ignore if they wanted to be successful.

- **Price thresholds or ceilings.** What do people expect now in terms of what they can or should pay to solve their problem? Are prospects anchored in terms of what they'd pay to have their problem solved? We once had a group of research participants tell us "I wouldn't pay more than $15 per month for this content because I already pay $10 per month for Netflix." We were testing a career-related content service. This was enlightening because we believed we would be compared to career related books and training budgets, not subscription streaming services. It helped us understand what in the pocketbook we'd be compared to and what we needed to overcome if we wanted to be outside that price anchor. This isn't meant to stifle your innovation or scope. It's merely a consideration as you think about your price value equation.

  Let's return to our fitness application example. We learned about the concept of industry-specific baseline expectations the hard way. Most exercisers were used to checking in for a class at the studio's front desk. In all our infinite wisdom, we thought we'd remove what we believed was an inefficiency by checking users in automatically via geofencing tech (a fancy term for technologically recognizing that your phone is geographically close to the studio, and doing something cool). Well, we learned that many exercisers left their phone in the car while working out in the studio which, depending on the parking situation, created some challenges for this brilliant idea. The point here is to understand the customer's prevailing expectations, habits, and processes, and the root causes behind them. In this case, there was a need to store the phone securely and that wasn't something we wanted to tackle in the early days of the app's development. The issues with using this tech (geofencing), if the exerciser left the phone in their car, led us to abandon this feature and go old school (we would guess geofencing tech is better now). Instead, we focused energy on the studios' application interface for checking-in exercisers for a class.

- **Look for Hacks.** Hacks are workarounds that seem to solve the problem perfectly in someone's eyes, but still pose a great opportunity for innovation. For example, Heather cooks quite a bit and she gets frustrated when cutting up veggies and scraping them into a small bowl. The veggies go everywhere but in the bowl itself. She learned a little hack from one of her friends: she'd turn her cutting board so that the handle (which is usually just a hand-sized hole at the top of the cutting board) was sitting over a small bowl. Then she'd scrape the veggies over the opening of the hole and voila—no veggie pieces left behind! Yes, it's trivial in the grand scheme of things, but if we were a cutting board producer, what an opportunity! And guess what, cutting board companies now build cutting board systems with perfectly sized detachable "catcher's mitts" for easy scraping and storing and raised the price of a common cutting board.

What hacks do you see your customers using? What little time-saving tricks do they use aside from your solution or in place of a solution altogether? Be open to seeing workarounds. Sometimes they don't jump out at you.

Needs come in all shapes and sizes. Always be on the lookout to identify needs when interacting with your prospects and customers. We've found that, as a guideline, most of the time you will find at least three to five prominent needs you must address in a solution for any single persona. Each persona may have the same set of needs, but the prominence of one need over the other may vary widely across personas. So, make sure you're keeping each list of needs clearly associated with individual personas. This is the first step to individualization of needs. This is where our qualifier "individualized" comes into play. We'll explain more shortly.

WHAT NEEDS ARE NOT

There are two things that always trip people up when we talk about identifying and taking action on needs. And they both have to do with the way a need is documented and communicated, and therefore, acted upon.

Needs Aren't Features or Solutions

This is the number one issue we see with the concept of uncovering needs. We see a list of "I need...." We all have a tendency to proceed straight to features or solutions because as product leaders, we are problem solvers. Please refrain from this tendency. Pause and take time to articulate a need before jumping to solutions.

Let's revisit the need we discussed earlier for Melanie: "I won't travel more than 2 to 3 miles from work or home to work out at a studio." That's the need. We could have said "We need our app to show only fitness classes or studios within 3 miles of the user's location in the search results." Which, okay, is a possible solution for the need. Sort of. But it shortchanges the wide-sweeping impact of the need we identified.

Instead, if we focus on Melanie's need, we learn that she needs classes that are close to her home or work. Focusing on her need forced us to change our studio recruiting strategy in the target county to ensure a critical mass of fun fitness classes where the persona (Melanie) lived. It narrowed our studio lead generation efforts to specific boroughs in the county. Even more specifically, it prioritized our studio recruitment efforts within each borough. If instead, we had merely worked to narrow our search results by default, the search results might never have revealed enough classes. We would have had great search tech, but not enough classes in the results to drive usage.

Let's take it one step further. What if the root cause behind the persona's need for a 2 to 3-mile limit on distance was that the average traffic patterns in the county meant that a 2 to 3-mile distance equated to a 20 to 30-minute commute during the 5:30-6:30 p.m. rush hour time, a popular exercise time for the Melanie population. And that the 20 to 30-minute commute made it almost impossible to take classes during that hour, unless Melanie left work early. Those search result filters don't look so great anymore, do they?

The point is you must explore different ways to address the persona's need and its root causes before presuming a solution. If you document and communicate needs as features, you'll defeat yourself before even getting out of the starting gate.

Needs Aren't Benefits

This mistake is very similar to translating needs directly into solutions. Before we jump into the feeling or benefit the persona wants to achieve, we must look without bias at the insight or need. Don't get us wrong— the benefit helps you understand what the persona is trying to achieve, but the underlying reason for not being able to achieve that is what facilitates focus and enables action. Focus on the underlying insight or root cause of what you are observing or hearing before jumping to a solution or end benefit.

WHY INDIVIDUALIZED NEEDS ARE IMPORTANT

How do you know what to work on first for any given problem–persona combination? Can you and your team agree on a path and stick to it without overturning decisions later? Defining the Problem Statement and the Persona is your north star. That's your starting point: the prioritized set of needs corresponding to a specific problem–persona combination gives you the path to a solution that delights the customer, provides the guardrails, so to speak, for the areas to focus on or avoid when solving for that problem and that persona. It ensures your focus for ideation and feature tradeoffs, whether it be your first version or your next product release.

After we provide a quick summary of four reasons that the Problem Statement and Persona elements of the Groundwork are so vital for both B2C and B2B design, we'll walk you through a detailed example.

Needs Enable Confidence in Early Feature Tradeoffs

Doing the Groundwork to identify and prioritize needs surrounding a specific problem for a given persona allows you to quickly say "No" to certain features or exploration. You can easily justify to leadership why you didn't pursue a particular feature area with a statement like "Jackie's primary needs are X and Y, which is why we focused more on these features and tabled these other features for now." It keeps the tradeoff discussion out of "opinion land" and solely in "customer-data land."

Needs Enable Clear Prioritization of Your Time

When you know and agree upon the prioritized set of needs for your persona(s) your team has the permission to focus their time on what matters most. Providing focused ideation time, testing, and iteration around the most important aspects of the solution. Which said a different way, you aren't spending time on random, broadly scoped aspects of the solution that are less likely to drive delight. It's the other side of the "Saying No" coin.

Needs Enable Faster Time to Market

Because you can confidently make tradeoffs early and test and iterate on only what's most important to your persona(s) you're able to avoid the delays that come from endless feature debate, overturned decisions, and designing or testing things that don't impact the delight of your primary persona(s). This dramatically reduces your cycle times and your overall release cycle.

Needs Minimize and Potentially Eliminates Costly Rework

Finding that you didn't hit the mark on the most important needs of your persona after you've built and released your shiny new experience is painful. Doing the Groundwork reduces the pain of rework after you release. We've all spent a lot of sleepless nights agonizing over something learned soon after release that seemed so obvious and could have been identified early on had we just developed a set of Individualized Needs.

Now let's look at an example of defining and prioritizing needs. The scenario involves a consumer product, but don't be fooled by the B2C example. This lesson is every bit as applicable to B2B product teams, and we'll talk more about the B2B implications in a bit. This example brings together all ingredients of the Groundwork—the Problem Statement, Persona, and Needs—to show you how they work effectively together to help make durable, confidence-inspiring decisions.

Imagine you're on the product team at a small, regional wagon manufacturer with a best-selling children's wagon. You're investigating ways to grow beyond your existing children's market and you've identified an opportunity to access a completely new set of customers.

The Problem Statement (using the Convergent Problem Statement Template we gave you earlier):

City-dweller-weekend-warriors want to feel freedom on the weekends through mini-adventures **but can't do this** *without a ton of pain and delay in mobilizing all their adventure gear,* **which happens** *when they are packing up and transferring their equipment from their apartment or storage unit to their car (and back)* **because** *the distance is long, and they have to take multiple heavy trips back and forth before all their gear is packed in their car.*

The Actionable Persona: (This is an extremely short version for illustrative purposes only. Do not try this at home (insert winking emoji).)

Jackie, a city dweller living in a high-rise apartment building in the Pacific Northwest, who goes on 2 to 3 weekend outdoor adventures a month.

As a product team within this wagon company, there are quite a few design elements to consider in solving Jackie's problem. Pragmatically, you can consider things like the following:

- Structure and Materials
  - Size and shape of the wagon
  - Durability
  - Water resistance
  - Compartments
- Movement and Maneuverability
  - Method: Motorized or manual
  - Wheels: Size and materials
  - Turning method: Motorized or manual, handle size
  - Turning radius
- Footprint and Storage
  - Collapsibility
  - Collapsed size

By the way, we're not saying that you can't build a hovercraft that operates via a smart speaker. We're merely providing a starting point for illustrative purposes. Now, how does knowing only the problem and the persona help you prioritize or focus on any one or one set of those design elements? You certainly could guess, but ideally, you'd have a set of prioritized needs to round out the Groundwork and establish a feature and design path before diving in.

Let's say you do some combination of five observational sessions and interviews. (See the **Practice II: Conducting Scrappy Research** chapter for why five is the magic number and how themes are identified.) Through that research, during which you interacted with your customer, your team identified some themes related to the problem of transporting recreational gear. You then translated those themes into needs for Jackie (the persona):

- *My parking spot isn't close to the elevator in my apartment building so I have to carry several loads quite a ways.*
- *Parking spots in my building's garage are tight, making it hard to maneuver big loads of adventure gear in and around the cars. My car is next to a pylon, so I have to back into my space that butts up against a concrete wall, making access to my trunk difficult.*
- *My elevator is usually filled with lots of people, so moving around and carrying big loads of stuff is a hassle.*
- *I'm usually carrying at least 40 lbs. of odd-sized stuff, including groceries, an ice chest (which is sometimes wet), big water containers, plastic gear chests, a tent, and so on.*
- *I'm often carrying my stuff on the sand, dirt, or gravel to get to my spot at a campsite, park site, or beach site.*
- *I live in an apartment building with little storage space; I have a small storage closet on a separate floor from my apartment, and my bedroom closet, which is full at the moment.*
- *My sister has a wagon she takes the kids to the park in. I think she paid under $100. It's not ideal; it has a hard shell and doesn't maneuver well, but it's better than nothing.*

This gives you a better picture of Jackie as it relates to her packing up for weekend adventures. And it sets you up to decide where to invest time and energy in solving this problem for the Jackie persona. But what if the persona was someone who didn't live in a high-rise apartment building but in a condo complex instead? A street-level duplex? What if the persona was a man or someone with a disability? Different combinations of problem-persona would yield different needs and a different prioritization of those needs. This then would yield different solutions or features of a solution.

And what if we told you that not all needs are created equal? Some are more pervasive (across the market base of Jackie's) or more frequent than others. Some, while less frequent, are highly painful. For example, Jackie's top two needs, based on the pervasiveness and frequency of the need, were the parking spots being very tight and the lack of storage in and near the apartment. You could probably imagine where you might start ideating. But what if the most pervasive or most pain-causing need was carrying the load on rough terrain? You can envision a very different approach to innovation, design, and feature prioritization depending on these factors.

In addition to identifying and documenting needs for any given problem-persona combination, you can see that roughly prioritizing those needs clarifies decision making. We'll talk more about how to do this later, but for now the point is that needs are a critical part of the Groundwork. Having a problem and a persona alone is not enough to define the best solution.

Needs are a necessary part of the Groundwork for any successful product creation or development process. Needs make decisions easier, they make decisions durable, and they minimize massive rework when solutions are scoped incorrectly.

Note to the B2B gang: We often see major B2B organizations struggling to make product and experience tradeoffs. There are a lot of opinions across the organization because the organization has many teams that each serve different personas, like buyers versus different users of the experience. It can be tough to get anything done without organizational churn. We see a lot of organizations completely paralyzed by the numerous competing opinions that are all based on knowledge of different problem-persona combinations. We promise that if you have a well-defined problem, a prioritized set of actionable personas, and a prioritized set of needs for each persona, you will find decision making smoother, more durable, and much easier to communicate. Think of this Pillar of the Groundwork as an insurance policy against significant rework costs later on and sleepless nights.

SUCCESSFUL IDENTIFICATION AND PRIORITIZATION OF NEEDS

Okay, let's talk about how to identify and prioritize needs successfully, leading to a set of individualized needs. This will yield the ability to confidently make tradeoffs early, spend time on ideas and product development that most impact the persona, and reduce, if not eliminate, costly rework.

Individualize the Needs

Most teams will identify a set of customer needs that span across multiple segments. They find and solve those needs that are penetrated the most across multiple segments to give their company the biggest chance at sales. Because, hey, you're bound to get some users when you're talking to a bigger market. So, why limit yourself to just one segment of the market? When companies do this their customer experience becomes diluted or bloated with lots of features that solve for many segments and become complex for any one user to use. So, in essence, the product experience is just okay (if you're lucky) for many but terrible for one.

By the way, this is not just a B2C phenomenon. Like B2C teams, most B2B products have different personas for specific task areas within the product, not just the buyer and user. User roles within a SaaS product is an example of this. The SaaS products often don't know who to solve for first and how to approach the design for any one user as they are trying to meet the needs of multiple segments to ensure the biggest market opportunity. So, this happens to product teams in any industry and product category. Without exception.

Most of the time, product teams have a long list of needs to address across multiple personas and they build a feature list that's equally long in an attempt to serve as many segments of the market as possible. What you end up with is feature bloat, a complex user experience, and extremely frustrated users.

We avoid the long lists by individualizing the needs; identifying and prioritizing needs for each persona within a particular problem space. Conduct the research and translate the needs for each persona in isolation before presuming a need is pervasive across multiple personas or has the same level of prioritization across personas.

Let's go back to our wagon example. So far, we have the Jackie persona. What if we had another persona, Michelle, who earned slightly more than Jackie and doesn't live in a high-rise apartment building? She still lives in an urban setting, but she lives in a street-level townhome or a small condo complex. Here's a list of her observed needs:

- *My parking spot is different every day because I park in the street and parking can be pretty far from my house. I'm often traipsing my stuff in the rain and snow to get to and from my car.*
- *I usually have to navigate a set of stairs and a couple of curbs to get to and from my car.*
- *I'm usually carrying at least 40 lbs. of odd-sized stuff, including groceries, an ice chest (that is sometimes wet), big water containers, plastic gear chests, and a tent.*
- *I'm often carrying my stuff on the sand, dirt, or gravel to get to my spot at a campsite, park site, or beach site.*
- *I don't have storage space. I have a one-car garage that doesn't leave much room after my husband's car is in the garage. I also have a small storage closet outside the building.*
- *My sister has a wagon she takes the kids to the park in. I think she paid under $100 for it. It's not ideal; it has a hard shell and doesn't maneuver well, but it's better than nothing.*

As you can see, Michelle's individualized needs overlap somewhat with those of Jackie, the original persona we discussed earlier. But Michelle has some unique needs that should also be considered.

If Jackie were your priority (maybe because the size of the customer base represented by that persona is significantly larger than that representing Michelle's persona, or if Jackie's persona has more strategic value to the company) you might prioritize the list of needs across the two personas differently than if Michelle was your priority. Right? You might also decide to prioritize one of Michelle's needs above a lower-priority need of Jackie's so as not to eliminate your opportunity within the Michelle base.

Understanding each persona's individualized set of needs allows you to make conscious tradeoffs and have a clear understanding of the impact your product or feature will have on each persona. If you lumped together all the needs observed across multiple personas within one problem space, the tradeoffs are much murkier and the impact of those tradeoffs is harder for the product team to understand.

Find the persona that clearly emerges as who you believe will drive the most revenue to your company, and another persona as a close second. You could first make decisions about features and designs to address the primary persona's top needs. And your team could consider the secondary persona's top one or two needs. Even if you can't optimize for both of the personas without creating feature bloat, you could get a head start on your secondary persona's needs. This is a balancing act that is far easier to navigate if you understand all the dimensions you need to balance and the implications of each decision you make on your primary and secondary personas.

Do the Research

A lot of teams have members who consider themselves target users and develop a solution based on their own relevant needs. That concept may help get you started with hypotheses, but you must validate those hypotheses by rolling up your sleeves and doing necessary research. You must research each persona to find a solid set of needs from which you can confidently make feature and design decisions.

In addition to what we talk about in the Practice II: Conducting Scrappy Research Practice chapter, we must add one thing now: observational research is very helpful at this stage. Observing people in their environments is the best way to discover relevant needs pertaining to the problem at hand. We are constantly reminded through our research that what people say they do and what people do are hardly ever the same thing.

When it comes to needs, observing your persona within their environment yields a much more informed set of needs than presuming one of your employee-users represents your target persona base, or that what your persona tells you is what the persona actually does. We understand it's not always possible, but whenever it is, conduct in-person, on-site observational research. See it with your own eyes!

Prioritize

Individualizing doesn't just mean having a set of needs by persona. It also means you're prioritizing those needs for each persona. Not all needs are created equal. Some are more pervasive. Some are more painful or prohibitive in terms of completing a task. Some are significantly more costly or more strategic to address. Too often, we see teams go headlong into developing features that are less important to the persona than other features, but are flashier in terms of marketing headlines, or have simpler implementation. Teams will add those features so they can say the product has more value than the alternatives. They end up spending less creative time on the things that matter, a product with more bells and whistles, and complexity in the experience that leads to customer dissatisfaction.

Prioritizing needs is key. At the end of the day, you and your team will have to make tradeoffs in features and scope. A thoughtful and agreed upon prioritization of needs by persona will allow you to make tradeoffs with confidence and efficiency. Prioritizing doesn't preclude you from addressing more needs to add more value to the product, but you'll at least know where to focus your effort first and foremost, and you'll get the most bang for your buck.

We'll talk more about how to prioritize, what criteria to use, and what prioritization looks like a bit later in this chapter.

Write in the Persona's Voice

You may have noticed that each of the needs lists we discussed was written in the customer's voice. We used their vernacular and conversational tone. It forces simplicity, which allows for broader team understanding and reinforces the connection to the persona (empathy with the persona). One of your goals as a product manager is to maintain a connection with the persona you're solving for. Without maintaining that connection, you and your team will have a longer, harder road in solving the original problem or delivering delight.

Writing in the persona's voice also forces you to feel what the persona feels and articulate needs from their perspective, rather than articulate your own interpretation or opinion of what you observed during your research. Let's face it, as product people, our job is to translate what we hear into action, and anything we can do to minimize bias keeps us on track.

The next time you're listing the observed needs, force yourself to write in the person's voice by asking "Would [insert persona name here] say this?" Make sure you isolate needs by persona before jumping into features that solve a problem for multiple personas. Even when you start with hypotheses, make sure you do the observational research to uncover the most important needs that may or may not validate your hypotheses. And keep your team focused on the highest priority needs so that you and your team make effective trade-off decisions.

GROUNDWORK IN ACTION: INTUIT

We love this story from Jessica Barker, VP and Segment Leader for TurboTax at Intuit, a company that's known for its obsession with delighting its customers and, as a result, outperforming its competitors in most spaces. So, when Jessica shared an example of how important it was to understand specific problem-persona combinations before tackling a market solution at large, we knew it would be a great lesson to share with you.

TurboTax, the tax software that serves over 30 million tax filers, enjoys one of the highest Net Promoter Scores in software today. It's well known for its simple, interview-style user experience and its refund calculator. TurboTax led the market with this user experience, which is why many digital tax solution companies have followed suit. The TurboTax product team was originally focused on individual tax filers and always knew that the self-employed market (people who file a schedule C form with their personal taxes) was a lucrative opportunity.

They set out to learn more about that market and identified a persona within the self-employed population that they called the "on-demand segment," or what we now might call the gig worker. These individuals were working for companies like Uber, TaskRabbit, and DoorDash. They began to identify this persona's needs.

What they learned was that gig workers weren't familiar with the concept of self-employment as it related to their taxes. They didn't think of themselves as self-employed. Most of these folks actually had other sources of income via W-2 wages. They treated their gigs as side jobs, but didn't realize the IRS considered earnings from their gig work as self-employment income.

The product team focused on the on-demand segment persona and their specific needs, believing that it would scale to the broader Schedule C market, outside the gig worker population. They solved for the gig worker extremely well but found their solution didn't address the needs of the broader self-employed population very well. They had oversimplified the user experience. The gig economy population was growing, but their needs didn't overlap as much as expected with the broader self-employed population that was much larger.

They stepped back and learned about the other segments. They took a deeper research dive into segmentation of the self-employed taxpayer market, looking for gaps in the current customer experience and also segmented the needs to better understand where the opportunities were. What they learned was surprising.

Other self-employed segments like consultants, for instance, realized their Schedule C income was a sole source of income. These individuals thought about tax implications year-round and most made estimated tax payments throughout the year, forcing them to budget and manage their finances differently from the gig worker. They had a perception that self-employed individuals were audited at a higher rate than the rest of the population. And these taxpayers made decisions weekly, if not daily, about whether to commingle personal and business expenses and cash flows, in fear of being audited. This made taxes feel much more onerous, and the complexity of their filings meant a higher likelihood of mistakes along the way.

On the surface, the gig worker and the consultant both had to file

Schedule C tax forms and although the calculations worked in much the same way, their situations, attitudes, and hence, their needs were significantly different.

The TurboTax team took what they learned from this research and leveraged machine learning models to create an industry assessor for the self-employed experience, which helped identify problem areas for the taxpayers. They built functionality into TurboTax to show taxpayers what deductions they might be missing, given their industry. They also trained their TurboTax CPAs (available live through the application experience for real-time questions) to be well versed in Schedule C filers and associated industries so they could help these individuals with specific tax questions. The new experience was a hit!

Jessica's team had identified a problem and solution that they believed would work at scale, but they were wrong. By looking deeply into the different personas within the self-employment market and identifying and prioritizing an expanded set of needs, they were able to evolve and scale the solution. She shared this example as a reminder that the work of understanding needs is most effective when you have both a clear problem and a clear persona.

GROUNDWORK IN ACTION: STARSONA

Peter Karpas has had a lot of key roles in the software industry. We both had a chance to see his leadership in action when he was chief marketing and product officer at Intuit back in 2007. Since then, he's had leading roles at PayPal, Xero, and First Data. We chatted with him about his latest endeavor, Starsona, an application where stars can offer personalized digital swag to their fans. What existed previously were charity auction sites where people would bid on things like video messages from stars.

When Peter's team started out, they wanted to understand the different segments of stars and their fans. There are some pretty distinct segments; take the differences between stars like Beyoncé or The Dollyrots. I bet you can recognize one of those names! To be clear, they both have passionate fans but the scale of fans and their interactions with fans are very different. As such the stars' needs are very different. Here are some examples:

- While Beyoncé values her fans, her direct interaction with any one of them, beyond a concert is rare. For The Dollyrots, their popularity (and their income) is directly correlated to their direct interactions with fans; and their fans telling others about them. Beyoncé probably went through this phase as well, but I think we can all attest to the fact that she's well beyond that point in her business.
- The structure of a star's business with fame like Beyoncé is also much different than that of a band like The Dollyrots. Beyoncé has multiple business managers for different aspects of business whereas stars like The Dollyrots might not even have one manager. A site that monetizes digital swag and personalized interactions would require a significantly different marketing strategy if you were trying to connect with managers versus directly with a star.
- Beyoncé's threshold on pricing for a single interaction is significantly different than that of The Dollyrots. The charity auction sites we talked about earlier had fans bidding $10,000 or more for a single personalized message from stars as big as Beyoncé. Whereas The Dollyrots are actively looking for multiple ways to interact with the public to build up their fanbase and revenue. Working with an app like Starsona that could open up more access to them, personally, was a need, not a gift or obligation. By the way, the fan that can afford $10,000 is a much smaller segment and probably expecting different experiences than those that are looking for something in the neighborhood of $50-$100.

These are just a few examples of needs of the different star segments and how they could dramatically change the business model of Starsona. As Peter's team's mission was to "spread happiness across as many people as they could" and make an impact in as many stars' revenue and relationships with fans as possible, they decided to focus on the 99%

of stars and not the 1%. Even if this might lower their revenue per star relative to the auction sites we talked about, it helped them focus on the needs of the smaller, eager stars that survived on direct relationships with their fan base. That's one decision down.

Peter's team decided to focus even further as the needs of stars within the 99% ranged dramatically. For instance, a sports star had different needs than a band had versus a YouTube star. The ongoing interactions with fans varied for each of these segments and the ability to get traction in those interactions with fans required different product decisions.

YouTubers, for instance, already had a full mobile set up for recording personalized digital messages easily. They just needed a venue to sell them. The deeper Peter's team got into the needs of each of the star segments the clearer the focus became.

As a result, their earlier focus was on YouTube personalities and bands (who also had a regular presence on YouTube and other video-driven social media). It allowed them to focus first on a mobile app and specific features that catered to folks that already had immediate capabilities of recording personalized messages with little to no effort. And while they are expanding from here, this early focus on the individualized needs of this narrow set of personas enabled them to move quickly and get early traction in the market.

Peter told us "people don't like to choose...great product managers choose!" This is so true. It's about deep investigation into the needs of multiple segments, understanding the implications and the prioritization of these needs and making the tough calls to focus in order to get traction quickly, learn quickly, and expand from there.

HOW TO PRIORITIZE NEEDS: THE FINAL STEP IN INDIVIDUALIZATION

The Individualized Needs Pillar of the Groundwork is not easy to grasp and can feel very nuanced. So, we're going to go deeper into an example to demonstrate how needs can be prioritized in an actionable way.

The key to successful prioritization is agreeing with your key stakeholders on which criteria you'll use to prioritize and having an effective team discussion around how each need addresses each agreed upon criterion (more on that shortly). While there isn't one way to do this, we have a simple model for you to follow that's tried and true, and a simple way of agreeing quickly on priorities.

We like to use four criteria to judge the priority of any given need. Bear with us, because we don't like making this too science-y with too much math, but we do believe more structured criteria drives good team discussion and shared commitment over the final prioritization. Note that we said that we want to drive good team discussion, not drive the decision. The criteria and process we discuss here are ways to structure conversation with your team so that together, you will agree on and commit to tradeoffs. Why will our strategy work? Because you'll all understand how you got to the tradeoffs you'll make. It's not about the numbers, per se. Let's dive in.

Below are the criteria we believe are most important in prioritizing needs and structuring conversations, and the recommended weightings for each criteria. It's your call if you want to change the weights, but we find that this framing yields successful prioritization conversations and results that teams can commit to. Before you change the weights, promise that there will be no tie scores in the weighing of each criterion. Ties only make the discussion and decision process murkier. Be bold—make a call. Think and rate each need against each of these criterion in isolation and in the following order:

Level of Pain (40%)

From the persona's perspective, does this need make the problem extraordinarily painful for them? How does it impact their ability to achieve their goal within the problem space you're in? Pain could mean anything from time-consuming to frustrating or confusing, or costly, and everything in between.

Rate each need on a scale of 1 to 10 in terms of the level of pain the need causes to the persona in and around the problem you are solving.

Note: Don't get wrapped around the axle on the 1 to 10 scale. More numbers make it harder to get a shared vision with your team. Consider scales like 1, 5, 10. The goal is to use a few numbers that are widely-enough distributed to result in needs with scores spread across an adequate range to make discussion easier. You don't want to end up with one need at a priority score of 5.986 and another at 5.987. That won't make discussion easy, and these scores are a tool for discussion. The need that ends up with the highest score represents a complete showstopper in accomplishing the persona's goal as it relates to solving the problem at hand, and the lowest represents minimal impact.

Pervasiveness (30%)

Does this need happen every time the persona is experiencing the problem you're solving? Does it happen to everyone in the base or just a subset? Think about frequency and coverage. If you have data, great. But more often, you'll have to use your gut and discuss it with the team. Put a stake in the ground and state a hypothesis that the entire team can commit to based on the best available data and agree on how and when you'll evaluate that hypothesis. You want to have a discussion with your team and come to some agreement on how pervasive the need is for the persona.

Rate pervasiveness using the same scale as you did for the level of pain. The needs with higher numbers of pervasiveness are those that everyone has or that happen every time they experience the problem. If you don't have data, use your gut based on the research you've done so far or use a viable hypothesis and test.

Cost (20%)

We can never avoid the cost question. Here, you want to go beyond just dollars. Think about political costs, environmental costs, technological costs, organizational costs, cultural costs, and the list goes on. What would it cost to address this particular need? Think broadly about what it would cost to address the root cause (or symptom) of the need you've observed.

Use the same scale, but reverse the ratings here. The highest number will represent a minimal cost, and the lowest will represent an almost impossible cost; what you would consider cost prohibitive.

Strategic Impact (10%)

The final criterion is what we call the strategic impact of addressing the particular need. If you were to address the need well, would it provide a competitive advantage for your business? Would it positively impact another product or business market position within the company? Would it get you closer to your company vision faster?

The highest number here would represent the largest strategic or competitive value to the business. Again, this is about the discussion and perceived value by the team. If you can get numbers on revenue value, time to market impact, etcetera, great. But those numbers are not required.

Let's apply this criteria in an example. We'll start by giving you a Problem Statement and a list of needs uncovered from research with our persona Melanie, who you met in the Persona chapter, and who had a problem related to exercising. We spoke of some of her needs earlier in this chapter as well. To kick this off, here's a Problem Statement that follows our Problem Statement Template:

> *Avid outdoor female exerciser (Melanie) wants to function effectively day-to-day and needs to feel motivated to work out,* **but she can't achieve this** *due to her monotonous exercise routine,* **which happens when** *she is stuck doing the same activities at her studio* **because** *her studio, though she loves it, focuses only on a single activity and her monthly fees for that studio make it hard to afford excessive drop-in fees for studios offering different, and new exercise activities to keep her inspired and working out.*

The persona's needs uncovered are as follows:

- *I need to be outside (from persona definition; see Figure 3-1).*
- *I won't buy before I try.*
- *I won't travel more than 2 to 3 miles from work or home to workout.*
- *I often don't decide what to do for my workout until mid-afternoon.*
- *I usually don't know what time I'll get out of work—it's not a 9 to 5 job.*
- *I need to get my sweat on so I feel like I worked out.*
- *I won't do an activity more than 2 times per month.*
- *My iPad is my computer.*

Let's select one need from this list to demonstrate how we use the scoring scale and the criteria weightings to prioritize the need. We'll start with "I usually don't know what time I'll get out of work—it's not a 9 to 5 job." For kicks, we're using a scale of 1-10.

Level of Pain (40%): Rated 10
Melanie couldn't predict what time she'd get out of work, and because desired studios fill their classes up earlier in the day, she loses out on reserved spots in fitness classes. This often leaves Melanie going home without exercising or doing something that she was less enthusiastic about. All of this led to fewer consecutive days of working out; a key metric of success for our solution. You could say that this lack of being able to reserve a spot due to the unpredictability of work was extremely painful, and therefore extremely relevant to our ability to solve this problem well.

Pervasiveness (30%): Rated 3
From research, we predicted that about 20% of the Melanie base had jobs that inhibited them from planning (e.g., late meetings, shift change responsibilities, evening reporting requirements). So, while the need scored high on the level of pain scale, it didn't on the level of pervasiveness.

Cost (20%): Rated 2
Our early research led us to believe the cost to address this need was potentially high or even impossible. Based on the research, we had a few hypotheses for why Melanie didn't plan. One of them was that she worked in a profession with "softer" quitting times due to late meetings, unpredictable shift changes, etc. Trying to get all our Melanies to change jobs wasn't going to happen. We also heard a desire for spontaneity, as Melanie wasn't sure how she'd feel at the end of the day. Maybe we could game the behavior to encourage planning? Maybe we could get studios to change class times? Any one of these ideas were potentially costly, in terms of both our time and our effort.

Strategic Impact (10%): Rated 7
Addressing the unpredictability of Melanie's schedule wasn't necessarily strategic. But knowing that the unpredictability drove lower reservation

behavior, and figuring out ways to drive usage despite that unpredictability would be critical to our long-term success and could drive a competitive advantage because there wasn't anyone that was doing this well at the time. Let's look at the weighted score of this need in Figure 4-1.

FIGURE 4–1

Overall Weighted Score

LEVEL OF PAIN	40%	*	RATING OF 10	=	4.0
PERVASIVENESS	30%	*	RATING OF 3	=	0.9
COST	20%	*	RATING OF 2	=	0.4
STRATEGIC IMPACT	10%	*	RATING OF 7	=	0.7
			Need Score		**6.0**

You'll want to do this exercise for each of the needs uncovered, then sort and see what falls out. Gut-check the results with the team. Does it feel right? Did you expect a different need at the top? Why isn't that the case? Does anything unexpected tell you something about how you are weighing your criteria? Or how you translated the need? It's not the template and detailed analytics, but the scoring and weighting that will facilitate a structured discussion.

Once you complete scoring for your first problem-persona combination, you have arrived at an individualized set of needs. Now, on to the next persona and their needs. This prioritization exercise is particularly important for B2B teams. The number of personas can overwhelm a B2B product team, making durable tradeoff decisions efficiently and confidently extremely difficult without this exercise. We usually recommend starting with a rough prioritization of personas. In every case we've seen, teams have an idea of which personas are more important than others based on either their strategic value to the company, the size of the base, the short-term revenue, or other factors. If you don't have an idea, put a stake in the ground given the data and company strategy at hand.

Once a team can agree on loose prioritization of the personas and a prioritization of needs, making the hard tradeoffs becomes a heck of a lot easier. Whether you're solving a particular need that overlaps all personas, or you're cutting a feature that doesn't positively impact your primary persona, you'll have an agreed-upon framework to make those decisions quickly and durably. With this comes an ease in justifying and communicating your decisions in a way that the leadership team can commit to.

SUMMARY

Let's recap.

- Needs are aspects of the problem, for a particular persona, that must be addressed as you define the solution to that problem.
- Needs must be defined and prioritized for each persona separately (a.k.a. individualizing those needs) before effective tradeoffs can be made. The assumption is that your team knows who the most important personas are and can make decisions confidently once they set prioritized needs by persona.
- Needs are obtained through research and observing a persona's environment as it relates to the problem you are solving, their process for getting tasks done, and their emotions or challenges in achieving their goal as it relates to the problem at hand.
- The team must agree on the list of prioritized needs. People will commit to decisions if they understand how you got there and were involved in applying the criteria to the various needs. Involving the team as much as possible in needs identification, translation, and prioritization is critical to gaining commitment.

You'll know you hit the nail on the head with your list of needs if the following are true:

- The needs are individualized by persona.
- The needs are customer-backed and empathy-based.

- There is shared agreement on the criteria used to prioritize the needs.
- The needs are known and agreed upon by the key stakeholders.

■ ■ ■

PART II

THE PRACTICES

5

INTRODUCTION TO
THE PRACTICES

IF WE asked you to name the most important practice a product management team should develop muscle strength in, what would you say? Why? Would it help the team move faster? Ensure a higher quality of products? Promote customer delight? As product leaders, we all focus our coaching efforts on those skills that we believe are nonnegotiable and we share these practices with us to each organization we build or lead.

We'd like to add three core practices to your repertoire to help you establish the Groundwork. Here's why: What if there was a way to ensure your team was always customer focused, that you made decisions with the customer in mind, and to increase your confidence in every product and feature you launch? Well, there is.

Through our experience, we've found that these three practices make all the difference when applied regularly and consistently to the three Pillars of the Groundwork. We see elements of these practices in leading companies that understand that highlighting and celebrating the practices is what sets the company apart. These practices will not only serve you well when establishing the Groundwork, but beyond that, they're useful in *every part* of your job as a product leader.

WHAT IS A PRACTICE?

Before we share these practices, let's start with a definition that we stitched together from various online sources[12]:

> *A practice is the actual application of an idea, belief, or method. To practice is the activity of doing something over and over, so that it becomes habitual, regular, and increases proficiency in the practice.*

We're highlighting three practices that should be part of every product manager's daily life. Whether developing product strategy, undertaking product discovery, or launching a new feature, each practice is relevant. You'll get better at deploying the three Pillars of the Groundwork as you implement these practices in almost every aspect of your job.

BENEFITS OF THE PRACTICES

When organizations lack these core practices, we see decisions overturned, lots of grumbling from development teams because direction constantly changes, slow progress because teams aren't focused and unhappy product teams who feel overwhelmed. Who wants that? The three practices bring you the following benefits.

Clear Focus

Deciding what to work on is always hard, no matter who you are. For product managers, decisions are exponentially more difficult because

---

[12] Sources include: mirriam-webster.com; macmillandictionary.com and yourdictionary.com

they have so many choices of what to build—every idea represents new work. The three practices help you narrow options and focus to provide a clear rationale for decisions.

Decisions That Stick

There's nothing worse than making a product decision and then having it overturned a few weeks later because there was a better idea, or a compelling sales call, or a really unhappy customer who demanded action. The three practices help you stay the course, stay true to your decision, and provide stability for the team.

Engaged Development Teams

When teams understand both what and why a decision is made, they are more committed, they offer suggestions, they care. The three practices help you communicate your decision process. Sharing that information with development teams increases engagement because the background and rigor of product decisions are clear.

Leadership Buy-In

Market data, and competitive analysis, and customer surveys are subject to interpretation and disagreement. Just presenting data is often not that useful or successful as a basis for getting leadership commitment. The three practices help eliminate arguments, enhance team commitment and promote supportive leadership.

AN OVERVIEW OF THE PRACTICES

Let's get into the practices! The three practices are the core techniques for developing a strong, customer-driven product management team:

- **Practice I:** Developing Hypotheses
- **Practice II:** Conducting Scrappy Research
- **Practice III:** Getting Commitment

Let's briefly look at each one.

Practice I: Developing Hypotheses

Product managers almost always work with ambiguity. They are constantly learning from customers, the market, and competitors. They're dealing with customer complaints, satisfaction surveys, and business metrics. They're bombarded by ideas from senior management, from their development teams, and from technical support. They are inspired (and driven) by products they admire, and what the competition is doing. There is never a shortage of opportunities and ideas. Where they choose to focus is critical.

Hypothesis-driven product managers understand that when they take time to carefully plan what they pay attention to and bravely uncover what they understand the least, that they can make decisions faster and more effectively.

The Developing Hypothesis Practice provides a discipline that helps the most meaningful ideas and problems naturally rise to the surface. After all, why would you spend time trying to learn anything you already understand? You want your teams to tackle the hardest problems first, and to have a clear line in the sand about what they believe and why so that they can move fast.

When you develop hypotheses, you have a consistent way to describe *what* you expect to be true, *why* you expect it to be true, and then outline how you will *learn* and provide evidence to support your belief. Presented with a hypothesis, product leaders and executives can give feedback, can partner with and coach you, and can give you additional context or information, outlining what else you may need to be aware of. You are partners in the work, aligned in a way that's rooted in the customer or business's problem.

Practice II: Conducting Scrappy Research

This practice is how you find the fastest, most convenient way to prove (or disprove) a hypothesis. Research can be a daunting task. In large organizations, entire teams focus just on customer research or just on market research. Research teams are skilled in analytics, have post-graduate degrees in human factors, and they run focus groups and massive quantitative surveys. Scrappy research isn't about any of this.

Scrappy research is the act of learning fast. It's guerilla tactics—getting to a customer or a proxy quickly and learning from them firsthand. When you couple this practice with the practice of Developing a Hypothesis, you get small, logical, hypothesis-driven experiments, which produce results that give you direction. There's no better way to make a product decision than by testing first and testing small, with customers.

An organization that embraces scrappy research as a practice understands the power of hearing from customers and infusing customer insights into *everything* they do, not just the big stuff.

Practice III: Getting Commitment

The third practice promotes getting buy-in to the decisions you make and the solutions you put forward. This practice can seem a little more elusive, but we are going to break it down into steps anyone can work through to get extraordinary results. Product managers who consistently practice getting commitment are seen as influential, they get things done, their teams love working with them, and they seem to have few to no barriers between themselves and partner groups within the organization. Executives outside of product management point to them as examples of great employees. If this sounds too good to be true, then you'll love this practice. You don't need to be born with charisma to get commitment using this practice.

The practice of getting commitment involves selecting the right customer data to share, identifying key stakeholders, developing a story, testing your story with a trial balloon, and sharing the results. Yes, there are a lot of steps to getting commitment, that's why we offer this as a practice. Once you master this practice, the results are magical. We promise!

HOW TO HELP YOUR TEAM DEVELOP THE PRACTICES

As with any practice, getting started isn't easy, and developing the practices so that they become habits is even harder. If you're a product leader reading this book, how can you help your team develop these practices? We've taken a page from practice and habit research to help your teams advance.

Set Expectations

Set expectations with your team that these practices are important. Build practices into personal objectives and hold your team accountable. Observe their attempts at implementing the practices, provide your feedback regularly in your one-on-ones, and ask questions about how their practice is going. What causes setbacks? What are they struggling with? Be an active participant in helping your team develop the practices by communicating expectations.

Frequent Repetition

Set aside time to discuss the practices in your weekly meetings—showcase examples of how the practices turned into a decision or a follow-up activity. Have your product managers take weekly turns describing their work in building these practices. Your prioritizing of this work in weekly sessions reinforces that you think it's important to develop these practices. Your product managers will feel compelled to do the work if they are expected to present results in a team meeting!

Tell Stories

Find ways to showcase the work your team does and describe the results of these practices. Connect the dots for why decisions are made and highlight how the decisions came about due to the core practices that the team demonstrated. Tell these stories regularly in team meetings or at company-wide meetings. Even tell these stories in executive sessions and offsites so that your peers will share and retell the ways your team gets results. This is a great way of getting additional support for your product managers.

Rewards and Recognition

A surefire way of getting people to do the work you want them to do is to reward them. Whether that's a simple thank-you, one-off rewards, or a bonus tied to objectives. Use whatever recognition systems your organization has in place commensurate with the results of these practices.

SUMMARY

We expect these three practices to be applied consistently and infused into every part of your job—weekly at a minimum, but great product teams engage in these practices daily. You'll see these practices applied to every Pillar of the Groundwork, and we'll explain in detail how to develop them, their practical application, and we'll describe examples in the coming chapters.

The practices of Developing Hypotheses and Conducting Scrappy Research are powerful and simple. They don't take much time and can be easily integrated into your teams' work. The Getting Commitment practice is layered on the others. It's how you get buy-in and approval for the data-backed decisions resulting from the first two practices. Implementing the third practice often requires the most leadership support and guidance. If you're a product leader, prioritizing Getting Commitment will accelerate the development of strong leaders within your company. It's worth taking the time. If you're a product manager, ask for feedback from your manager as you work on these practices. They'll want to help.

■ ■ ■

6

PRACTICE I: DEVELOPING HYPOTHESES

REMEMBER BACK in high school when you grappled with a scientific hypothesis? If you don't that's okay, here's the dictionary definition[13] to jog your memory:

> *A supposition or proposed explanation made based on limited evidence as a start point for further investigation.*

Scientists use hypotheses to state what they think will happen, and then they conduct a series of experiments to prove or disprove their expectation. Vidya remembers this experience from high school:

> *Back in my tenth-grade science class, I developed a hypothesis that plants would grow better if they "listened" to music. I set up two plants of equal size and health and I put one in the living room where it was exposed to general conversation, some*

television, and not much attention, and I put the second one in my bedroom and played music constantly. I watered them at exactly the same time and I took growth measurements over two weeks. I remember being overjoyed to have an excuse to blast my music at all waking hours, but not much about the results to be honest. However, I still remember the tenets of a good experiment; I started with a testable hypothesis, and an expectation of the results, and then I went about controlling variables so that any results could be attributable to the conditions of my experiment.

Most of us have lost sight of what a hypothesis is with that level of understanding and control. If you're in software, you're well versed in a term called a/b testing. This type of experimentation is a method of comparing two versions of (usually) a web or app page to see which one performs better. This type of experiment is often set up to see which page converts more visitors into buyers. By putting up multiple versions of a page, companies can continuously optimize. For companies that introduce a/b testing with real rigor—a specific hypothesis with an expected outcome—this type of continuous testing can drive appreciably better results.

Even when companies engage in a/b testing, there's often no rigorous hypothesis that initiates the test. And for the majority of companies that conduct no a/b testing, we have very little in the way of hypotheses-driven processes. Much of the time, companies introduce features, modifications, and even new products, without some simple hypothesis testing that could save time and avoid unnecessary work across the board. Teams get pulled into an endless cycle of doing more and more work without pausing to understand if their work will produce the results the company is looking for.

Our version of a hypothesis is formed as a simple if, then, because statement:

---

[13] Oxford Dictionary

If... *[specific, repeatable action]*
Then... *[expected, measurable outcome]*
Because... *[clearly stated assumption]*

This practice is important to every assumption you make as you build your product. Instilling this hypothesis discipline across your teams will bring extraordinary results.

WHAT A HYPOTHESIS IS NOT

A quick word about some bad hypotheses we've seen and what you should be wary of at all times:

A Known Fact

We already talked about being careful not to test things you already know. We've seen teams spin up and run tests where anyone could have predicted the results. Why do they do this? Sometimes it's because someone told them they needed proof. If someone tells you that, just do the market research, or dig into existing customer data.

Find the proof that already exists within your company; you don't need to expend resources running a test. Sometimes it's because someone forces the team into constant testing, and the team has no time to think, so they resort to testing ideas that they already know work. If this sounds like you, then ease up on your testing—you're in a death spiral. It's better to test once every two weeks, taking the time to develop a hypothesis out of big assumptions and get meaningful results, rather than stick with weekly experiments because that's what the process dictates.

We often like to have teams list their riskiest assumptions, those that scare them the most. It's a great place to start writing a hypothesis, because the results can have a dramatic impact on your business. Make sure that with any hypothesis you or your team write, you can't wait to get the results!

HOW TO AVOID THIS TRAP

Look at the converse, if you had already proven that the hypothesis was not true (invalidated) would you be working differently?

A Way to Make a Decision

Be careful not to make big decisions based on the results of testing with a hypothesis and obtaining one outcome. We've seen leaders make significant business decisions based on the results of a single experiment. A hypothesis and subsequent results give you data. This data needs to be seen in context and verified with additional experiments. Think about what it means for an outcome to confirm your hypothesis. What other factors impacted the result? How do you test those variables? It's exciting to have a strong hypothesis and confirm it. That should set up the next several experiments and hypotheses to validate the result. Stay skeptical and ask more questions. If the outcomes are validated, you have strong evidence to support the next steps for your team, for the company leadership, or for the board.

By the way, we are not advocating endless research. We are advocating educated gut instincts. Meaning, make decisions based on the data you have and move forward with the intent of continuing learning to validate your decisions and any additional hypotheses uncovered through your research. You don't want to get stuck in an endless cycle of research without progress. The point is to establish a hypothesis, do scrappy research to learn, make a decision, and move forward with any hypothesis that was confirmed or falsified; constantly checking your gut throughout focused hypothesis-driven learning.

HOW TO AVOID THIS TRAP

Be wary of making decisions based on one hypothesis and one set of results from one experiment.

A Question

A hypothesis states what you expect to be true. Whether the experiment results in a positive or negative outcome, you have a logical, rational reason for what will happen, why it will happen, and how much impact it will have. None of these are questions; they are statements based on what you know and have learned. Don't ask open-ended questions with hypotheses. Use hypotheses to declare a direction that moves your product or feature forward. If after you have the results from your hypothesis you still have a lot of unanswered questions, you probably need to do some more scrappy research (see next chapter!). The bolder your hypothesis, the more structured your tests and the clearer the results.

HOW TO AVOID THIS TRAP

Take a position with your hypothesis, don't straddle the middle ground.

Don't Have A Laundry List of Hypotheses

We asked you to not make important decisions based on one hypothesis and one experiment, but we also don't want you to be stuck in a never-ending situation with one question leading to another and so on. Don't create endless lists of questions to drive multiple hypotheses that will end up paralyzing you into not being able to make any decisions. What we're looking for is a small set of hypotheses, that if proven false would dramatically change your path of action. You might face a lot of doubts or questions from your team, or from other managers. Focus on the most important hypothesis that keeps you up at night, test it, then move on.

HOW TO AVOID THIS TRAP

Remove all hypotheses from testing that aren't mission critical.

Use these four tips along with the six characteristics we shared earlier as a quick checklist to test whether you have a strong hypothesis.

WHY A HYPOTHESIS IS IMPORTANT

As you may have figured out by now, everything we espouse is based on understanding the customer. It's hard to find a company that will tell you that they don't want to hear from customers. And that makes it hard to develop good hypotheses about who they are and what they need. But companies can demonstrate a big failure point in execution when they conduct customer research. These companies will say they talk to customers all the time but what we see is a big gap in understanding what customers are saying. Let's talk a bit more about what this may look like:

> Company A is a large consumer business. They have a research facility that conducts customer research like clockwork every two weeks, putting every feature of their product through some sort of customer testing. They have a dedicated customer research analyst who talks to customers and develops reports. All the reports go to a shared storage where anyone in the company can access them.

That scenario might sound like magic to some of you, but we hear the slasher sound from the movie "Psycho." We see three red flags: 1) A dedicated research team, someone outside the product team, does all the research; 2) Research is a stage of the development process; 3) Reports that don't have a clear recipient. Let's examine each red flag a bit more to understand why this is a nightmare-inducing situation for us.

A Dedicated Research Team

Large companies can afford separate research departments. This is great—having people with the right skills and knowledge to do all sorts of deep research is a gift we would never turn down. However, when external research departments want to control all customer research, as often happens, it's a problem. Most specialized departments end up wanting control, which is not necessarily a bad thing. A specialized department can manage its work more efficiently, can force a company to prioritize, and can see connections between the different products and user experiences the company offers. But when a product team loses all ability to do their own customer research, it creates a chasm that is not easily crossed. A dedicated research analyst should, at the very least, be dotted lined into the product team, they should know exactly what the product is designed to do and why, and they should take their direction from a product manager. If these steps are in place, then the centralized research department becomes a benefit and not a curse.

Research as A Recurring Process

Whenever we hear that research is done regularly, we dig a bit deeper. What drives the cycle of research activity? Is the research focused around a hypothesis, or is it happening because it's an activity to check off the to-do list? While we encourage frequent research, it should always be attached to something that the PM needs to learn in order to make a decision; the research should always be done with an actual target or goal in mind. All research should start with a hypothesis. If you consider research as a regular occurring activity, go back and review what the inputs and outputs are. Ask yourself if you're getting value from the work that's being done.

Zombie Reports

What does your research report look like? Is it updated from a template? How much is customized? Does it include quotes, pictures, and videos? Ask yourself: *Does it provide insight?* We both have had the experience of having dedicated research groups added to our department. These researchers would present the team with PowerPoints of their research every two weeks, like clockwork. Those reports provided a lot of colorful images of customers who the researcher had spoken to, a lot of background information, and summaries of their discussions. Our teams would dutifully listen to the presentation, some would read the report and every person would file them away and they'd never be referred to again. When you receive a research report, are you doing anything with it? Does it live after the meeting? Does your team use the research results to shape their work? Were you able to make a product decision on the basis of the research? If not, stop the madness, cancel the report, save time and effort. Ask your team to provide a hypothesis, and then leverage your research resources to learn and validate or invalidate the hypothesis. Every research activity should produce results that the team needs.

We're going to keep talking about hypotheses in relation to customer research because it's easiest to see how introducing this practice can have an immediate impact. Most companies conduct some sort of customer research, and we see over and over again that it's not optimized to give them actionable results, partly because they don't start with a solid hypothesis. We're determined to fully persuade you about the value of hypothesis testing!

Let's explore the four clues that tell us a company is making the most of their customer research and what it looks like when they don't have a hypothesis-driven culture.

All Customer Testing Starts with a Hypothesis

When you put your idea, prototype, or even your product in front of a customer without having any expectation of what they will do, the resulting response or behavior can be interpreted to mean anything and you can have wildly different responses. Here's some examples to illustrate what we mean:

- *The customer missed seeing a screen.* That's okay, we'll provide the information again in a later part of the process. *OR* We better make that screen mandatory, so they can't move off the page without acknowledging they've read the terms.
- *The customer said they hated the color.* We better change the colors because we don't like them either. *OR* The colors are part of our brand, let's ignore this feedback.
- *The customer said they liked the concept.* Awesome, let's launch! *OR* Good to know, let's see if they equally like this next concept.

Any result can seem important, any result can seem insignificant. *What you give meaning to drives action.* If you need to, require that for six months, your team must get your approval before any research project begins. Force your team to tell you the exact reason for conducting the research; what hypothesis are they trying to evaluate? Why is it important to learn in the stage of product development they're in? What do they plan to do based on what they learn? If you're excited about getting the results, you know the research matters.

Bottom line: If you have no hypothesis for customer testing, there is no point in doing it. That's right, we said it. Don't bother doing customer research if you don't have a hypothesis. It's a total waste of the team's time and the customer's time.

Writing Down A Hypothesis Enables Focus

Most of us spend a lot of time in meetings sharing opinions when we review customer research. We make a lot of assumptions, and we tend to hear what we want to hear. We're sure you've been in more than one meeting like this. Many companies are so execution-focused that they move from one activity to another, without taking the time to help teams align, ask the right questions, and facilitate real collaboration. Here's an example:

> *Company B is a fast-growing online retailer. They've embraced a/b testing and they have all the right systems and processes in place to immediately execute any test that anyone in the company dreams up. As soon as enough data is collected, they can end the test and then reset to get ready for the next test.*

When we see a situation like this, the first question we ask the development team is "Do you know why this test is important?" Unfortunately, most of the time, the answer is an embarrassed "No." They conduct tests without knowing why they're important, or what outcome to expect.

If you want your entire team on the same page, you have to start with carefully constructing and sharing why the test is important. We know that this is time-consuming, and writing a hypothesis is not easy. However, sharing this information ahead of time invites the entire team to participate through offering suggestions, including new testing ideas, and engages them to care about the results.

Share What You're Trying to Learn and Why

So many teams just execute tasks, without understanding why they're doing the work. By simply writing down the hypothesis, you immediately connect your team with a shared purpose and not just an activity.

Hypotheses Improve Learning Outcomes

Any time you or your team learns from customers it's a good thing. However, a focus on constantly learning can also backfire without some simple steps to prioritize the most important things to learn and understand why they're important. Having a hypothesis helps you prioritize to optimize the time and effort you spend on learning. Here's what this might look like:

> Company C is a B2B business that has a large portfolio of goods they deliver directly to their customer. They support their customers through multiple channels. They capture all the customer data that comes in through voice and chat channels and they send out a summary to everyone in the company. Every week, the CEO shares a highlight of customer feedback. Customer quotes are posted on the walls. The company prides itself on being customer centric. All customer feedback makes its way to the product team, who captures all the information in the form of user stories, and enters the stories into their backlog. Without fail, they capture all customer data.

While this might sound great on the surface, the results can be dire for the organization. When all customer data is important, each piece of data can translate into an update or new idea—and that leads to a potential endless list of tasks that can occupy the team for months or years. The reason is that without a hypothesis, all data can seem important and it's hard for anything (except major bugs) to stand out as substantial. Having so much customer data can be overwhelming to manage, and impossible to use for guiding decisions. Although capturing all the data may seem like it promotes important learning, the data becomes noise.

Focus on What Matters

Hypotheses are critical to understand what key pieces of data the team should tune in to, and those pieces of data will serve as signals for further, deeper research. A hypothesis helps maximize learning from customer data because it filters out the critical from the trivial, the signal from the noise.

Hypotheses Enable Impartial Decisions

A good hypothesis cuts through debate. When you engage in the practice of developing a hypothesis you avoid the need to get to consensus, endless discussions with no decision, or a top-down mandate being forced on the team. Setting a hypothesis and then reviewing the results, helps give direction. In our experience, a company caught in debate without direction looks like this:

Company D is a B2B organization that serves large institutional clients. They have very strong leaders that lead sales, account management, and customer service. Each of these leaders, and their teams, talk to clients and learn from them continually. Every group has strong ideas of what their client needs and want to make sure that those needs are met. Cross-functional team meetings are noisy debates with each group arguing that their approach is best. They often run out of time to make any decision in the meeting, which makes the next meeting even more charged as the urgency to solve for their customers keeps increasing.

We've seen this situation a lot, especially when you have well-meaning and customer-focused teams. Adding the simple discipline of asking teams to bring in a hypothesis creates a consistent structure to enable constructive debate and to prioritize consistently. And then, once the hypothesis is tested, results can be reviewed and decisions made. Now that we've convinced you that developing a hypothesis is a valuable practice, let's talk about how you go about creating one.

WHAT MAKES A STRONG HYPOTHESIS

In this section, we're going to describe what makes for a strong hypothesis. We are constantly inspired with new product ideas—whether that's through customer observations, the competition, or an "aha!" moment in the shower. Every idea has the potential to be formed into a hypothesis. The way to ensure you have a strong hypothesis, one worthy of testing, is by reviewing that they conform to these six characteristics:

Logical

This seems obvious, but think about the number of times someone has a good idea on the team. Good ideas are a dime a dozen, sadly. We've seen multiple teams become overwhelmed with new ideas entering the system because they see a competitor launch a new feature, or because an investor or senior leader gets inspired by the latest shiny object. Being logical means that there is clear, sound reasoning connected to the hypothesis. The idea doesn't come from left field; you can point to evidence to suggest the outcome will be promising.

Testable

Making sure a hypothesis is testable is one of the hardest aspects of generating a great hypothesis. Often, teams feel like they need to fully build and launch their product to get actionable data so they forgo hypothesis testing altogether. While your results may not be statistically significant, think about how you might, with minimal resources, prove that you're heading in the right direction.

Think of Vidya's plant experiment we mentioned earlier. Knowing that the plant should grow 2 centimeters within two weeks made it possible to test musical enhancements. If the plant grew or did not grow significantly more than 2 centimeters, we would know if the hypothesis was true or false. With practice, writing a testable hypothesis becomes easier—teams get very creative and quickly adapt to creating small tests with minimal resources.

Precise

How you put together a hypothesis counts. Using deliberate words that indicate a specific outcome is important. Otherwise, any given outcome can be seen as either confirming or falsifying. Being precise means being crystal clear on what you're testing and why, and documenting the rationale for what it means to run the experiment, what resources you'll need to experiment, how long it will take, and when you'll know the results.

About Something Measurable

We need to understand which numbers matter before you do the research. If your hypothesis is that more visitors will see your webpage when you make a certain change, then you need to know exactly how many more must visit for the change to be meaningful, and thus, for the hypothesis to be confirmed. An increase of 1% may mean nothing to one company, and it may mean millions in incremental revenue to another. Understanding what measures are important gives you a good indication of whether the experiment or test should even occur. If the results can't confirm or falsify your hypothesis, why do the research? This is a hard characteristic to pin down, but it's critical to ask both if you know what the measurement is, and whether the measurement is meaningful.

Has an Expected Outcome

We want you to be able to explain with a logical, clear reason what outcome you expect. The line gets tricky here—if you already know the outcome, then go get the data to prove how you already know this. Why spend time testing things you already know? We see teams share hypotheses with us all the time about things they already know. They do this because it's comforting to be proven right. On the other extreme— if you don't know what outcome to expect, then how will you plan the precise experiment that could achieve that outcome and how could you know what to measure? Make sure your hypothesis specifies an outcome and that the outcome will address your hypothesis.

Falsifiable

The last of the characteristics is making sure that you can invalidate your hypothesis. The way to think about this is to make sure you don't set your research up in such a way that the results are subjective, or that you're not capturing the right data to be able to have a clear result.

These six characteristics are intended to help you coach your product managers. Instead of just providing feedback on a hypothesis (or rejecting it outright), point to one or more of the guidelines and discuss how their hypothesis may miss the mark. It's a teaching moment and a much more productive conversation at the same time.

THREE STEPS TO CREATING A HYPOTHESIS

There are three steps to get to a strong hypothesis: 1) Create a list of questions that outlines what you don't yet know that's important to know; 2) Prioritize items in this list based on what's most relevant and critical to your business; 3) Shape these statements and questions into well-formed hypotheses. Let's dive into each step:

1. Identify What You Don't Know

The best way to avoid some of the pitfalls we described earlier is to think about what you truly don't know about the customer or problem. What are you guessing at or making assumptions about, with regard to their behaviors, their needs or the problem they're facing? What conditions would have to be true for a new feature to work? If this is a new market, then what conditions need to be true for you to launch? If this is for a physical product, what conditions must exist for a customer to successfully use it? What assumptions are you making about your persona, that if proven false, would dramatically change your course of action? Have you accurately translated what a customer has told you they wanted into a need?

Each of these questions represent the types of assumptions we make every day. Most of the time we jump straight from idea or insight, right into development. This stage requires you to painstakingly face everything that might go wrong. We often start with asking ourselves the question "What would make this idea fail?"

Now write down everything you don't know as a question. Here's an example going back to Melanie, our Actionable Persona example. As we were considering her behaviors, we created a list, and here are a couple of the assumptions we made:

- Melanie loves to try new forms of exercise.
- Melanie won't care if she can't go to the same studio more than three times a month.

Those assumptions matter. We believe them to be true because we spent a lot of time talking with her, to develop our Actionable Persona. Both of these assumptions were driving major design decisions. We're taking this head-on, leaning into the biggest assumptions that will impact our business model. What we learn will help us make an important product decision.

2. Prioritize Assumptions

If you do step one thoroughly, you're going to end up with a lot of assumptions. Not all of the assumptions are critical and you want to know which will have the most impact on your business. We turn to a design thinking technique called a "bullseye diagram" to help sort through and classify all these assumptions. We like to make this a visual exercise that the entire team can participate in. On a large whiteboard draw three concentric circles, each one bigger than the last. Write each of your assumptions on separate Post-it Notes so you can move them around easily. Now it's time to prioritize.

You can place one assumption in the innermost circle. In the next circle, you get to place three assumptions, and in the outermost ring, you get a choice of five assumptions[14]. As you pick up each assumption, ask "how important is it to know this?" You can also set up multiple bullseye diagrams and have each member of your team run through the prioritization process individually, and then gather to compare results.[15] We've even invited key stakeholders in our business to participate so that we get to hear their thoughts and concerns. Consider what different perspectives you may want as you try to understand what's most important for you to learn. As an added benefit, it keeps everyone on the same page and increases commitment to, and interest in, the research you're about to start.

With this exercise, you'll have a list of prioritized assumptions—and a clear winner. This winning assumption is used for the first hypothesis you write.

---

[14] We use a 1-3-5 ratio to really force some tough choices. With new products/ideation, we may well have a ratio of 3-7-10. Consider what resources and capacity you have to do follow-on research. If you can only run one experiment with one hypothesis, don't give your team the choice of selecting more than one assumption as their top choice.

[15] This design thinking technique is terrific for all sorts of prioritization. You can change the number of items within each circle, just make sure there is a big contrast to force the right conversations around relative importance and impact.

3. Convert Assumptions to Hypotheses

This step converts the prioritized assumption into a hypothesis. Let's return to the hypothesis format we introduced at the start of the chapter:

If... *[specific, repeatable action]*
Then... *[expected, measurable outcome]*
Because... *[clearly stated assumption]*

The easiest way we've found to create a strong hypothesis is to start with your desired outcome. What needs to be true to resolve your assumption? Do you want 10% more sign-ups to your site? Do you want 25% fewer customer calls? Do you want to increase your NPS by 5 points? Whether it's 5 points or 10 points of NPS you're trying to impact, or 25% less customer contacts; pick a figure that is meaningful to the business and will make a difference. Start with your desired outcome and then pick the appropriate measurement.

Next, move to the clearly stated, highest-priority assumption. This is where you can rewrite and reshape your assumption. If you truly believe you can't make a significant difference by addressing this assumption, then move to your next ring of assumptions. There is no point in trying to create a test for an assumption that you don't believe you can tackle. This is where you need a strong understanding of your business, your customers, and your market. Know what is important, and drive to make an impact where it counts.

Finally, consider the test itself. What action do you believe will create a significant result? Do you need to make a change to how people sign-up for your service? Do you need to introduce a new offering? Do you need to increase loyalty with existing customers?

Let's go back to our Melanie persona and share our highest prioritized assumption, one that we believe is critical to our business:

Melanie loves to try new forms of exercise.

We believe that Melanie will love to try new forms of exercise. If that is true, we're going to give her many different classes to choose from. This will dictate how quickly we need to bring on new partners and it will dictate the design of our application. We want to make sure the assumption is true, so let's turn this into a hypothesis that we can test given what's important for our business:

1. Desired Measurable Outcome: We want Melanie to love trying new exercises so much that she will purchase at least one class a week. That will give us enough revenue based on our projected number of customers.
2. Clearly Stated Assumption: Choice is the primary driver of purchase.
3. Specific, Repeatable Action: We will display different classes every week to keep her interested and engaged.

This creates a hypothesis we can test:

If... we offer different classes per week to choose from
Then... we'll get at least one purchase
Because... choice is the primary driver of purchase

After developing this hypothesis, we created three different prototypes on paper to test the different ways that Melanie could choose classes and our hypothesis was validated. Remember, your assumption is always derived from something you don't know and your hypothesis is based on your belief that a specific action will deliver the outcome your business is looking for. We told you to start with the measurable, desired outcome. When you start with what matters most for the business, whether that's retention, or growth. Perhaps it's revenue. Home in on the metric you most want to impact.

Like any practice, getting results requires constant feeding and nurturing. Starting to build a hypothesis-driven organization is going to be ugly and painful at the beginning. At first, you won't get hypotheses that are elegantly formed and perfectly clear. A lot of them will be quite confusing and badly written and that's okay. Use this practice with every Pillar as you create Convergent Problem Statements, and Actionable Personas. Use the hypothesis practice to derive Individualized Needs. Pretty soon you'll find yourself in a hypothesis-driven culture, with a team that's always focusing on the riskiest assumptions, ready to make the biggest business impact.

A Note to Product Leaders: Make sure you ask your team for a hypothesis whenever they want to do research, whether with customers, online, or through a vendor. Set the expectation that you care as much about what they want to learn, as well as how they'll learn, and the results they achieve.

PRACTICE IN ACTION: STANDARD BANK

Standard Bank is a South African financial institution, which offers banking and financial services to individuals and companies in Africa. With a market cap of nearly $10 billion, they are Africa's biggest lender. We started working with Standard Bank in 2015 when they asked us to support their product team in building digital and mobile products. Joanne Norton is Head of Digital Product Management in the Digital Platforms Division of Standard Bank, and has worked in that role for over 8 years. She leads a team of digital product managers and designers tasked with translating customer needs into new digital products.

Joanne's team understands how to move through the product development lifecycle, starting with a foundation, then iterating and testing their way to a finished product. Most of Standard Bank's product line is in traditional banking with some innovative products built for mobile users. Our conversation was focused on how they leveraged foundational concepts to drive ideation. Joanne and her team had just launched a product that was born at a hackathon. Their version of a hackathon is a two-day event that brings product, IT, and development teams together to take an idea through to a testable prototype. The idea that won was a prototype that provided a fun banking experience for kids. When Joanne's team took on the winning idea, they went back to basics.

They started with a hypothesis about how people first became linked with the bank and how you could build ongoing loyalty through to adulthood. One of the first things they did was to bring a bunch of kids into a room, put their parents in another room, and start listening to feature ideas from both the children and their parents. Then they framed each feature idea as a hypothesis and tested it (through cheap, fast prototypes) with specific metrics (measurable, desired outcome) driving validation.

What was so interesting about this approach is once they confirmed each hypothesis, they knew they were onto something and got funding to develop some creative solutions that resulted in a visually exciting, interactive experience. Validating the needs of both kids and parents enabled them to create an experience significantly differentiated from any of their competitors.

We loved hearing that even with a workable and winning prototype, the Standard Bank team went back to basics to generate a set of hypotheses and develop tests in order to determine what age to focus on (9 years old), what the most compelling needs for both kids and parents were (thereby determining functionality for both users), and what truly made it sticky (fun, interactive, gaming concepts). Their hypotheses and corresponding measures are what the business uses today to drive metrics of success. A true hypothesis-as-hero story!

SUMMARY

As we come to the end of this first critical practice, we want to leave you with some feel-good moments. When you create a culture based on hypotheses and research you get benefits that are worth the effort.

Clear Focus and Direction

As product leaders one of the most important parts of our job is to make product decisions. This can either feel arbitrary and confusing, or it can be empowering and aligning. We choose to make it the latter. Teams collectively sigh with relief when leadership is aligned. A discipline of hypothesis-based testing shows that their leaders have a distinct and clear methodology for approaching their work. We feel joy when our teams ask us, "What's the hypothesis?" and we can share the question, the hypothesis, the research, the assumptions, and the rationale for why we believe we should move in any given direction. A culture of hypothesis testing provides ongoing focus and direction, giving attention and momentum to research and action.

Aligned Team

What's cool about product development is that it truly takes all parts of the team to develop and deliver a product. We want every person on our team to actively think about the results of their work. To do this, you need to share what you're doing and why. We highly recommend conducting the assumptions exercise as a full product team, collectively deciding the trickiest and most dangerous assumptions to tackle. You'll find that there is so much more buy-in and interest in the subsequent testing and research you do. Sharing what's important, and providing transparency for how you make priority calls and product decisions, sets the stage for a well-aligned team.

Cost-Effective Research

Finally, we all have limited resources, whether it's a budget, access to people, or time. Make the most of the resources you spend on customer research or prototype testing, and even building your product by insisting that all work starts with a hypothesis. You may well find that half of your backlog magically disappears when you more tightly control what flows into the backlog funnel, and when a validated hypothesis motivates all new products or features you build.

■ ■ ■

7

PRACTICE II: CONDUCTING SCRAPPY RESEARCH

WE LOVE research. Wherever you are in the product creation process, having mad research skills will set you apart from the rest and make your job a cakewalk. Well, we're exaggerating a bit, but good research skills will make your life much easier, not to mention much more fun and successful.

Heather was one of those kids who would grill her friends about their family vacations, in part so she could better plan hers, but also to learn more about what her friends liked to do. She was constantly curious. She always wanted to know how and why people did what they did, constantly probing, "Why?" She said she often got the eye roll. "Heather, stop asking so many questions!" To this day, she finds that her ability to express (and satisfy) her curiosity is one of the most enjoyable aspects of being a product leader and one of the reasons why, after working as a corporate executive, she directed her career toward leading new product teams and startups. She needed to get back to direct contact with customers and first-hand knowledge of problems her team was solving for.

We embrace a philosophy that ongoing scrappy research is the only way to infuse customer learning into day-to-day operations. That scrappy research is the only way to drive continued, forward momentum with confidence. It's a practice that we hold sacred and incorporate in every product management operating mechanism: strategy building, road mapping, product definition, feature definition, user story development, and so on.

To be clear, we are not talking about massive quantitative surveys or big qualitative studies that often take months from start to finish. We're talking about scrappy research.

Don't get us wrong; we believe in big, statistically valid, formal research. While it always has a place in our hearts, we know that we don't have the time or budget for it in our day-to-day product management jobs. So, what usually happens? Well, we either do a gut check and we move on or we vacillate with the team, back and forth between different opinions. Either way, not taking the time to gather customer insight is risky and painful. Big-pocketed organizations can do big formal research projects a couple of times a year. But most organizations may not even manage to do this once a year. As product people, we have to make decisions daily. What can we do outside of the big formal research fun zone to help us make good decisions?

That's where scrappy research comes in. To do the Groundwork necessary to build kickass products, you need a set of solid scrappy research practices. Most companies don't even test their ideas or designs; some companies do a/b testing. But even in those companies we see a lack of hypotheses-driven testing. A lot of the time, features, modifications, and even new products are introduced without some simple hypothesis testing partnered with scrappy research that could significantly improve outcomes. Teams get pulled into the endless cycle of creating more work—more features, more fixes, more big initiatives—without pausing to understand whether that work will produce the results the company is looking for.

This is how we define Scrappy Research:

A small number of structured customer interactions to test your most pressing hypotheses within five working days.

We'll break this down shortly, but for now, all you need to know is that it is fast, focused customer interactions to get you the input you need to make timely and durable product decisions.

WHAT SCRAPPY RESEARCH IS NOT

Scrappy research is not waiting weeks or months for an answer to big or small questions. It's about focused forward momentum. Let's talk about what scrappy research isn't.

Addressing A Laundry List of Random Questions

Too often teams can't decide what they need to learn first. They have a huge list of questions that they try to cram into big (and even small) research studies. This always slows the team's momentum, either when trying to agree on which questions to answer or when planning and finding the time necessary to get them all answered in an actionable manner. Scrappy research enables forward momentum in any given project or product creation process by focusing solely on the hypothesis at hand. You want quick, relevant, timely answers so you can keep moving. That means you'll have to turn away people with requests like, "Can you just add this one question to your interviews this week?" And you know that happens!

Worrying About Statistically Valid Sample Sizes

Many teams assume that they need 50 to 100 interviews under their belt before they can make accurate decisions. Recruiting that many people is costly; both in time and dollars. And because of this assumption in sample size, many teams just don't attempt it given budget or time constraints. This is a mistake.

Scrappy research is about conducting a small set of customer interactions with consistent format and with good hygiene. In fact, you only need five interactions to build an actionable set of themes. (We'll explain all that shortly.) With small numbers like that it's conceivable that you could do multiple scrappy studies in any given month or week. Your successful Scrappy Research Practice could depend on how many lunch breaks you're willing to give up to interact with customers. There were times where we could do one or two interactions a day if we had to—one early morning for East Coast participants and one at lunch or right after work for West Coast participants. It can be done!

Hiring an Outside Research Firm

Scrappy research can and should be done by you and your team. You can do it over lunch, over a team brown bag lunch, after work, before work, pre-scheduled as a regular item on your calendar. The point is, you and your team need to hear customer feedback firsthand and probe for root causes, and therefore, actionable results. Research firms aren't close to your business, they don't usually know where to probe, or what would be considered surprising, or where the true nuggets of learning are. Make the time.

Spending Big Dollars

Again, the perception that qualitative research requires large sample sizes, and therefore big budgets, often leads to bypassing research altogether. Scrappy research is cheap and simple once you set up a repeatable process, which we talk about in the coming pages. It's about you doing the work in quick increments versus hiring an expensive research firm that charges thousands of dollars for small sets of interviews. Hiring a firm also delays actionable results. It's usually 4 to 6 weeks from the first contact to actionable results when outsourcing this work. Developing a consistent, ongoing internal practice of scrappy research reduces both time-to-value and cost.

WHY SCRAPPY RESEARCH IS IMPORTANT

Scrappy research is a practice that turns product managers into great leaders. Let's talk about some reasons why.

Scrappy Research Prevents a Significant Amount of Rework

How many times a day do you make decisions about a product: feature prioritization, backlog cuts, design decisions, strategy decisions, and so on? Product people make scads of decisions every day based on intuition and whatever data they have (which can be none, depending on how big or how new the product or business is). Is it the best-kept secret that product people probably make most of their daily decisions based on gut feelings? Nope. That is our life as product people. Take this example:

> *Product Team A decides to build one feature instead of another based on what they think is the right direction. They build it with tracking so they can get usage data in real time. Within 6 weeks of releasing the functionality, they learn that the feature isn't used as much as they expected, and the desired business outcome isn't being achieved. The team reworked the functionality and relaunched within 12 weeks.*

On the surface this may look fantastic: They implemented tracking, they learned within 6 weeks, and had a new version out in three months. These are huge accomplishments for some companies, but we're here to tell you that this is an unacceptable cost of time and rework.

Keep this quote by Thomas Gilb cemented in your mind: "Once a system is in development, correcting a problem costs 10 times as much as fixing the same problem in design. If the system has been released, it costs 100 times as much relative to fixing in design."

Thomas Gilb is famous for improving organizations' delivery capability. Scrappy research combined with a clear hypothesis is a catalyst for reducing work. To drive faster success at a significantly lower cost, make scrappy research an ongoing habit instead of a special occasion.

Scrappy Research Enables Durable Decisions

Every product manager experiences an overturned product decision at least once in their career. We've all been there. It's frustrating. In some cases, we've seen that when product decisions are consistently overturned, it ends a career.

Product Manager A proposes a direction for a product to his leader and cross-functional partners. The product manager bases the logic behind his proposed direction on some big hypotheses, but he feels confident the hypotheses will prove correct, given what his customer service team has told him. In the proposal meeting, the cross-functional team seems a bit skeptical, but they all walk out of the room nodding and the development team gets to work. Two weeks later his leader calls him and says, "We need to pause work on this because your cross-functional counterpart isn't supportive of the direction and expects a different direction instead...and I think I might agree. Let's change direction."

Replace the word "direction" here with "feature," "design change," or "product trade-off." We've all been through a similar scenario at one time or another. Other people's opinions start to take over and you're stuck in the middle. For those of you who experience this as a norm, which it is in some business cultures, listen up—conducting scrappy research as a practice is for you. Whenever you need to change direction, implement a new feature, update prioritization of initiatives, or anything that you know may differ from the expectations your product team holds today, communicate your logic through customer-backed reasoning.

Scrappy research allows the customer to speak in lieu of anyone's opinion. Practicing ongoing customer-research, albeit scrappy, builds customer-backed logic that your team can understand and commit to. You may not get a consensus on your decision, but you'll get commitment because they understand the logic behind it. We call that *shared vision*. Yes, it sounds like bogus corporate jargon. We learned it early on in our careers from Steve Bennett, a former CEO of Intuit, who we both worked under. And it's one of the only corporate jargon terms we embraced. We love the term because it represents something more powerful than "consensus." Shared vision is our way of driving commitment. We could write an entire book on the importance of shared vision, but the point here is to get away from opinion and use customer-backed logic to communicate and gain commitment to proposed decisions.

Scrappy Research Keeps You Close to the Customer

This isn't a goal of scrappy research in and of itself, but it sure makes you a far more effective product person. You can make faster product decisions, gain the trust of your entire team and your cross-functional stakeholders, and feel more confident in your day-to-day operating role. It's win-win-win.

We can't tell you how many times we see product managers deferring customer understanding to others—researchers, business analysts, UX designers. Deferring is convenient and allows you to pile other stuff on your plate. And yes, it looks like you're making the right work prioritization decision initially, but you're probably not.

People distance themselves from their customers and spin their wheels with decision vacillation because the loudest opinion in the room generally wins. They can't effectively prioritize the backlog, they add a constant barrage of shiny objects, and they have no way to justify tradeoffs with confidence. All in all, the other stuff that you pile on your plate becomes significantly more time consuming. Scrappy research is not a full-time job, but it's a fundamental practice that makes or breaks a product person's career over time.

DEVELOPING THE PRACTICE OF SCRAPPY RESEARCH

There are a few things to keep in mind when developing a practice of scrappy research.

Focus on a Hypothesis

We won't repeat our last practice, but remember that scrappy research isn't like your annual surveys or studies where you ask a heap of questions that span across many aspects of the existing experience or the broader opportunity at hand. It's focused on what you need to learn to verify your hypothesis, which when verified, will allow you to take immediate action. Your hypothesis should always be the rudder of your customer interactions.

Use the Rule of Five

As part of our definition of scrappy research, we said you need only a small number of interactions. Math from world leaders in research-based user experiences says that five consistently structured interactions will uncover actionable themes. The goal is to get actionable data from the smallest sample in the shortest amount of time. Five is the target number. Our experience shows that as long as the other key elements of scrappy research, discussed below, are present, themes begin to arise after five interactions. If you don't see themes emerging by that point, ask yourself if any of the elements below are missing. If so, rectify that and add one or two additional interactions to correct the issue. Five to seven interactions is usually all you need for directional themes.

Use a Consistently Structured Format

Interactions must be consistently structured. What does "structured" mean? Well, the protocol you use for each interaction must be identical (interview, observational session, usability session, etc.). The questions you ask, the order in which you ask them, and the profile of the participant to whom you ask the questions must be the same for all participants. It doesn't have to be fancy, but it needs to be consistent. It's the only way you can generate actionable learning from such a small group of interactions.

Use a Well-Defined and Consistent Participant Profile

We use the term profile here instead of persona. A participant profile consists of any characteristics important to your learning goals. Sometimes you use scrappy research to learn who your persona is, or you are validating a particular behavior, attitude or characteristic of your persona. You may also be testing an idea with a new customer segment that might result in a newly defined persona. You may not always be talking to a person that has every characteristic you defined in one of your official personas. This is why we use the term profile instead of persona.

That being said, imagine you're talking to three different participant profiles within a set of five interactions. If you are inconsistent in terms of the participant profiles, one of two things will happen: 1) No themes arise across the five interactions at all or 2) One thing is mentioned twice by participants with the same profile, but not by the others. Is that data trustworthy as a theme? Would you feel confident taking action on that data? Would team members commit to an idea based on the data? Probably not. So, make sure you are clear about who your persona is (or the profile you want to learn about to determine particular characteristics of your target persona) and stick with it for all interactions within a scrappy research study. If you're a little unclear on who your persona is, that's fine. Just make sure you have the different potential profiles clearly defined and sampled into separate scrappy studies. Each set of five scrappy interviews must have the same profile.

Finish Within Days, Not Weeks

We say 5 days, but we've done this scrappy research within one day and achieved a reliable answer that enabled us to move forward with confidence. Over time, scrappy research should become an effortless practice that you leverage weekly, if not daily. Use it any time you have a hypothesis and you want to avoid opinion-based decision making and drive confidence among your cross-functional partners in the product decisions you need to make. Scrappy research should become second nature and repeatable as you get more experience at it.

Set Up Repeatable Participant Recruiting

One way to ensure scrappy research becomes part of your day-to-day operation, as opposed to event driven, is to figure out a way to have a constant pipeline of target profile participants. Successful companies like 99designs, who we mentioned earlier, leverage multiple channels they already have to connect with users. They implement and listen in on multiple customer feedback channels like Slack, support calls, surveys, and transaction feedback. All of their employees interact with business users and designers through these channels on an ongoing basis. Any of these methods are great ways to find participants for scrappy interviewing. Oftentimes, on surveys or support calls, the simple added question of "Would you be willing to have a short call with us to better understand your feedback?" opens up the door to someone itching to give you their feedback. Be creative with your recruitment.

For B2B, this is probably one of the biggest inhibitors to an ongoing scrappy research practice. We always hear "Sales won't let us talk to customers" or "Our client contacts won't let us talk to their users." We hear you, and we've been there. It takes time and resourcefulness to get the ball rolling. But once you identify a couple of ways to get access, you should accumulate a group of these folks as your *customer advisory group* and reward them generously for participating in periodic feedback sessions. Here are some ideas to consider:

- Solicit your customer base through periodic, already established user communications (we already mentioned a few channels).
- Ride along with your sales team to meetings with clients and prospects who meet your target profile.
- Listen in on service calls and ask customers if they're interested in participating in an interview.
- Leverage a recruiter, which can be costly for more niche profiles, but can be very effective and efficient.
- Use proxies like the sales team, customer service folks, and other people who interact frequently with your target user profile. We've even talked with outside folks who interact with our target profile frequently, like distribution reps, value added reseller reps, and service people. It's not ideal, but it's better than nothing as long as you understand the lens through which you're hearing the feedback.
- If you survey your base periodically, at the end of the survey ask "Would you be willing to have a short phone call to discuss your feedback?"
- Be creative! Use any channel you or a partner has to connect with your users or potential buyers. As long as the users fit your target profile (even a proxy with first-hand knowledge of these folks) you can keep learning!

For B2C, it can be simpler to find participants. Here are some ideas to consider in addition to what we said above:

- Intercept prospects in relevant places, like Starbucks, shopping malls, and event locations.
- Buy targeted lists.
- Advertise on Craigslist. Yes, sounds appallingly skewed, but we've had great success in targeted Craigslist recruiting with an effective screener survey.
- Recruit friends and family.

Regardless of how you do it, as you start to interview people, ask if they'd be willing to participate again so you can start building a database of participants that you can leverage in the future. Develop a repeatable process so participant recruitment becomes second nature to you and your team while building a pool of easy-access participants for ongoing scrappy research.

STEPS TO CONDUCTING A SUCCESSFUL SCRAPPY STUDY

Conducting scrappy research isn't hard. Here are a few easy steps to get you started.

Develop a Quick Plan

Your plan can be one page. Don't overthink it. Here are some basic elements of a good plan:

1. **Identify the hypothesis.** This is your research goal. Practice I: Developing Hypotheses should set you up nicely for this.
2. **Decide on interaction type.** We usually focus on one of two interaction types: interviews or observational sessions. There are many others, but we feel these are the easiest and fastest to do. There's very little set up required and if you have a solid set of interview questions (what we call an interview script) you can be on a call that afternoon getting your first set of data.
3. **Define who you want to talk to.** If you aren't sure who your target persona is, or you're testing to define your target persona, then define two or three distinct profiles you need to talk to.

Each profile would make up a separate scrappy study using the same interview script (5 interactions per profile).

4. **Create a script.** This is a fancy word for a list of questions or an agenda for the session. Here's a quick outline to follow:

   a. **Introduction:** Make them feel comfortable and set expectations.

   b. **Warm up:** Cover background questions and validate they are the target profile.

   c. **Deep dive:** Ask the hypothesis-testing questions.

   d. **Show and tell** (if you're testing a concept): Focus on hypothesis-testing questions, but with an actual concept.

   e. **Wrap up:** Set expectations for next steps and thank the participant. If they were a good participant (articulate and not afraid to give you their opinion) ask them if they'd be willing to participate in the future.

Find Participants

There are a lot of touchpoints in your company and a lot of places you can find prospective participants. Remember, you don't need a statistically valid sample size, you only need five to seven participants with similar profiles. Don't overthink recruitment.

Please don't forget to offer incentives to participants. Incentives are crucial to ensure your scrappy research duration lasts days and not weeks because without an incentive, you can't have confidence that your participants will show up. The more participants don't show up, the more your study drags out. We've tested a lot of incentives and found that motivating working-class participants to take an hour out of their day to chat with you requires no less than $50. We love to use $50 Amazon gift cards as incentives.

One more thing: Always recruit more participants than you need. The rule of thumb is 10 to 20% more participants than the number of interviews or sessions you need. This way you'll have backups in case you have no-shows and you won't delay your work by having to recruit again. If you find you don't need the additional participants, you can decide to interview those folks anyway (more data doesn't hurt) or politely thank them for responding and tell them you will be contacting them for the next round of interviews. Don't lose them as future participants!

Conduct Effective Sessions

To ensure you have an effective session, prepare yourself and your participants for great interactions. Send out a communication that sets expectations for what will occur during the session, how to enter into the interaction (call instructions, directions to your location, etc.), and asks for permission to record the session. Make it drop-dead simple for people to participate and put them at ease by explaining what you expect of them.

Don't forget to practice your script and make sure the wording is comfortable for you. You don't know ▪ how many times we see people fumble through an interview with a customer because the questions weren't practiced and were just too wordy or formal. That fumbling makes participants feel uncomfortable. So be sure to practice a couple times before you "go on stage." Here are a few pointers for conducting a research session.

1. **Put your participants at ease.** Many participants are nervous because they want to make sure they answer questions in a way they think you want them to answer. But you don't want them to overthink their answers. If they aren't comfortable, their answers will be subpar, and you won't accomplish your mission. Get comfortable with the wording and cadence of the questions. Your nervousness and lack of confidence makes your participant feel nervous and lack confidence. And for gosh sakes, make them feel like they're the hero. Because, frankly, they are. By giving you their feedback, they are essentially contributing to the success of your business.

2. **Be open to surprises.** Don't walk into a session with assumptions about how participants will answer. Assumptions bias your results and negate your entire research mission, which is to test a hypothesis. This means no leading questions, keep to open-ended questions, and push for root causes when you hear something you don't expect.

   One example is in Heather's experience as chief product officer for a digital healthcare startup. This startup offered a way for primary care providers to submit questions to specialists in support of treating their patients within community clinics. Patients in these community clinics had a tough time getting specialty care; lack of insurance, low income, lack of transportation, and the specialty care clinics that were overcapacity made getting specialty care difficult. So, giving primary care providers a way to partner with specialists electronically increased the likelihood that patients would get some specialty care input when needed. Heather and her team set out to understand specialist motivation around interacting with primary care providers for the concept they were testing. They believed that specialist motivation was going to be purely a reimbursement issue and were looking for a reimbursement amount at which specialists would engage in answering primary care provider questions. The team was determined to understand that economic equation and how to build an experience to maintain the specialists' motivation. Boy, were they headed in the wrong direction.

As Heather and her team started interviewing specialists they learned that, while reimbursement was important, the real value to the specialists was in teaching primary care providers how to treat health issues that they often referred to specialists but which were minor enough that primary care providers could treat them themselves. Referring patients with these health issues could delay care for weeks due to the challenges in specialty care access. Moreover, teaching primary care providers to treat these issues meant fewer patients taking up precious space in specialists' waiting rooms that could have gone to patients that truly needed specialty care (i.e., procedures that only specialists could do). The opportunity to train primary care providers, change their referral habits, and give them the confidence to treat these patients at the primary care clinic was hugely appealing, both financially and from a care standpoint.

The realization that the per transaction reimbursement wasn't the only value motivating specialists to participate on the platform changed how the team thought about the experience and the economic model for the entire business. Had they only focused on questions about the reimbursement model and not been open to other benefits to specialists, they would have continued down the product path of building a whiz-bang reimbursement transaction monitor that worked like a slot machine!

3. **Record everything.** If you don't have another person helping you in these sessions, figure out how to use recording devices to ease the load so you can interact directly with the participant without worrying about writing things down. Even if we take notes, we always use online video conferencing with recording capabilities or use an audio recording device. When taking notes, capture all observations without judgment. Judgment comes later, after all the sessions are complete.

4. **Lastly, make sure your script fits your session time.** A good rule of thumb is to make sure your intro, your full set of questions, and your wrap up takes no more than 60 minutes. It's a lot to get in, especially if you're testing a concept. Make sure you rehearse and give yourself a buffer for slight meandering when you hit a juicy insight and need to ask follow-up questions to dig deeper.

Ask Good Questions

Asking the right questions makes or breaks whether or not you meet your learning goals (proving or disproving your hypotheses) and also gain the insights you need to take action.

Ask Only Open-Ended Questions

Avoid single-word-answer questions. No duh, right? You'd be surprised what busy people sometimes throw into a script. They often forget this tactic and end up with very few questions that drive elaboration and finish their sessions with less than stellar results.

Poke and Prod Your Participants with the "5 Whys"

We don't mean that literally, but kinda. Just remember that the first answer out of a participant's mouth isn't usually an actionable insight. So, practice the 5 Whys. Simply put, the 5 Whys is an iterative interviewing practice for getting to root causes.

The technique was originally developed by Sakichi Toyoda and was used within the Toyota Motor Corporation during the evolution of its manufacturing methodologies. The architect of the Toyota Production

System, Taiichi Ohno (the father of kanban), described the 5 Whys method as "the basis of Toyota's scientific approach by repeating *why* five times to find the nature of the problem, as well as its solution..."[16] The 5 Whys probe what's buried under the participants' answers to get to root causes. We're not advocating that as you interview, you use the word "why" every time you get an answer from a participant. We want your participants to stay through the interview! Instead we're recommending you probe and ask elaborative questions like, "Help me understand a bit more about that....", "Tell me more...", "Can you elaborate on that?", and "What did you mean by that?"

In our experience, the true nugget of learning where the actionable insight exists and where innovation is most ripe, is at the third or higher level of elaboration. We can demonstrate this with a very simple example. In this scenario, you find out that your participant wants to switch to a software solution other than yours:

FIGURE 7–1

Why	You	Participant
1ST	WHY DO YOU WANT TO SWITCH?	*Because I'm frustrated with your product.*
2ND	CAN YOU TELL ME A BIT MORE ABOUT THAT?	*Well, I was on hold forever last week.*
3RD	WHY DID YOU CALL US?	*I tried to set up a report on my dashboard, but it didn't work. I tried for over an hour and followed your instructions, but it still didn't work. So, I called.*
4TH	CAN YOU HELP ME UNDERSTAND WHAT YOU WERE TRYING TO CREATE?	*I needed to create a report for my boss so he knew what the variances were in the most important accounts in the P&L.*
5TH	WHY IS THIS USEFUL FOR YOU AND YOUR BOSS?	*He has to know the variances often, well before the end of the month, because it dictates some of our buying decisions for inventory.*

---

16 Bryan Collins, A Remarkably Effective Problem-Solving Tool Anyone Can Use, Forbes Magazine; Forbes, July 17, 2018.

This example shows that you have significantly more to work with in terms of potentially stemming this participants defection after probing their answers a bit. You could have stopped at "I was on hold forever" and tried to solve the customer service issue. But digging deeper, you learn that your product is lacking a pretty key feature that would have voided the need to call altogether. What if that report was already available and they just didn't know about it? That would be a simple communication fix. What if that was a report that you've started to learn was important, but you haven't pulled the trigger because you weren't sure it was critical for users. There are a whole host of things that could be going on beneath the surface. Your goal is to probe and understand the root cause of the problem and take action on that, rather than just taking the first answer as *the* insight.

It may seem tedious to you, but you'll start to understand how valuable the digging becomes in building themes and being able to take action, confidently, on the small number of sessions you complete.

Use the Magic Wand

If you could wave a magic wand and change ONE thing about this [process, task, product, etc.] to make it [easier, better, more profitable, etc.], what would it be and why?

We ask this question to get an understanding of participants' priorities. If you're only asking questions like, "What would you change about this [process, task, product, etc.] to make it easier?" you might get a myriad of answers from each and across all your participants. And after five participants, how would you know which answer is most important? Even if one or two answers overlapped across all the participants, it doesn't mean they are the most important issues, it just means that everyone experiences those issues. So how do decide what to act on? How do you know what to put effort into?

This is why we focus on extremes in our questioning. Think about questions that force participants to think about the top, worst, best, most painful, and so on. The magic wand question and others like it uncover themes that help drive priorities based on a small number of interviews, which is the goal of scrappy research.

Focus on Research Goals, But Be Open to Meandering

Your questions should always keep the hypotheses you are trying to verify in mind. But as you probe you may find an interesting thread that reveals other insights related to the problem you are solving. Don't be afraid to spend some time learning, but make sure you bring the session back to the topic at hand once you understand that new insight a bit better. Remember, you only have five to seven interviews, so you need to make the most of these sessions!

Translate Results

This is one of our favorite parts of scrappy research. The unveiling! This is where the rubber hits the road. Whether it's rescoping your problem, updating your persona, or uncovering relevant customer needs, make sure you step back and remember why you did this scrappy research. What were you trying to solve? Focus on the hypotheses you set out to validate. Your analysis and presentation of the data should always center on this. Too often we see an outpouring of results with everything anyone said during a session, leaving the audience of product decision-makers confused and feeling like they were no better off than before they started. So, focus carefully on how you analyze and present your results.

Here are some tips on analysis.

1. **Focus on themes.** Themes are anything that was brought up more than two times throughout the sessions. Anything less than that is interesting, but not necessarily actionable. Therefore, add those possibly "interesting tidbits" at the end of your research results. We realize that these tidbits may lead you to additional hypotheses that warrant additional scrappy research, and that's fine. But your mission here is to focus on actionable learning vs. shiny new objects that are off-topic and not related to validating your original hypothesis.
2. **Review the data through three lenses.** Before you finalize your recommendations, review the data through these three distinct lenses, one lens at a time. You'll usually see different themes arise through each of the lenses:

a. **Persona characteristics:** Go through participants' answers with your persona or particular profile traits in mind. Did the existence of a particular persona trait (situational context, behavior, attitude, demographic, or other psychographic) dictate different answers to your questions? If so, why? Analyze themes that arise through the presence, or lack of, any particular persona trait. Maybe you're interviewing five to seven participants for each of your persona profiles. Or you may be testing hypotheses related to a particular trait within your persona profile.

For example, imagine one of your persona's behaviors is "I won't travel more than 2 to 3 miles to workout at a studio" (remember how important that was to our Melanie persona?). You would then look at every session through the lens of whether or not they would travel 2 to 3 miles or farther and whether that behavior correlated to different answers to your interview questions. Try doing that analysis with each important persona trait for each of your five to seven participants. You wouldn't do this with every aspect of a persona, but you do want to do it for the biggest-impact traits on which your team is basing their product direction.

Look to see if certain traits drive different perspectives or root causes of the problem. Look to see if how much value they put on solving the problem differs depending on the persona or a trait of that persona. Said another way, whenever you do see differences in the answers to questions, find out whether it's persona or trait related. What is it within a profile that drives a different perspective? This lens alone may allow you to confirm or falsify any hypotheses you have about your persona. It's the best way to evolve your persona over time. The more you view your data through this lens, the tighter the definition of your persona becomes.

b. **Hypotheses:** For each hypothesis you were testing, run through each session's data and confirm or falsify each hypothesis you're testing and the deep reasoning behind the results for each participant. What themes consistently arise across the sessions? What insights does this uncover in your persona? For your problem? Your persona's needs? How will this change your product direction, if at all?

c. **Willingness to pay or to take action:** At the end of the day, you need to know what will drive business growth. Review the data from the perspective of who will pay (or donate, or recommend you, or whatever action you want your customers to take) versus who will not. We simply annotate each set of session notes with the participant's willingness or lack thereof to pay (or take action) for what we were testing. We try to uncover what those who are not willing to pay have in common. Is there something about how they perceived the problem that reduced their likelihood to pay or take action? Is there something about their environmental context or behaviors or attitudes that affected that likelihood? What was different between those who were willing to pay versus those who weren't?

This might mean you parse the data between existing paying users and free users. It might mean parsing the data on willingness to pay for adjacent products or stated willingness to pay for a solution to their problem. Parsing the data according to whatever might indicate a customer's willingness to pay or take the desired action, always yields helpful insights. Ask yourself questions like: *What were the common reasons people objected to pay or take action? What were the benefits that people were willing to pay for and why? What does that tell you about the problem? The persona? Prioritization of the persona's needs?*

You may analyze the data through additional lenses, depending on your industry or market, but we always use at least these three. It takes some extra time during data analysis, but these lenses maximize how much you learn from the small sample size.

3. **Identify actions as a result of what you learned.** Make sure you clearly articulate what actions you propose. Tie these actions back to your original hypotheses and the actual insights you

culled from the research. Make sure these actions are clearly ownable with measurable milestones.

4. **Simplify your presentation.** We always recommend sharing your research findings with key stakeholders; decision makers and team members who are impacted by your resulting actions. Your presentation should be simple, often five slides max. Here's an outline that works well for a presentation:

   a. **Hypotheses:** What were the goals of the research?

   b. **Profiles targeted and research logistics:** Provide context for who you talked to, how you conducted this research, and why it's relevant.

   c. **Resulting themes and insights:** Report on anything mentioned across participants more than two times. These themes should represent what you learned (factual observations) and how it addresses (proves or disproves) any given hypothesis (your conclusions). Add any additional important themes you uncovered that might not directly address your hypothesis but try and focus on the goals you started with. Bring all this to life by using the customers' voice. Use actual quotes, pictures, or even a video from the sessions. Hearing directly from customers amps up your presentation substantially.

   d. **Interesting tidbits:** You can include anything mentioned that wasn't a theme but could be a thread to tug on later through additional research. This might be a surprise finding, or a potentially new problem or persona. Tidbits don't have to yield a conclusion or action, but they may be worth exploring later, and therefore, you want to highlight the information.

   e. **Recommended actions:** This is the most common thing missed when product managers present research findings. Recommended actions help the team with the "So now what?" question. Do we stop the development effort? Do we pivot our design direction? Do we add that feature? Do we have to think differently about our persona? What does all this mean in terms of what I do tomorrow? Tell your audience explicitly what you plan to do based on what you (and they) just learned.

PRACTICE IN ACTION: INTUIT

Remember the Follow Me Home program from the Groundwork Pillar II: Actionable Persona chapter—the observational research practice implemented back in the 1990s at Intuit? All business units at Intuit adopted this program as part of their day-to-day operations. That was our first foray into scrappy research. We included the extended functional team in those sessions; some team members even conducted sessions themselves.

We included engineers, customer support, research, product management, and more. Even Steve Bennett, our CEO at the time, participated in the program. It was a simple program: follow our customers and prospects to where the problem we were solving existed and observe them operating in their environment. It wasn't fancy. We identified these folks through our surveys, customer database, and customer support calls and invited them to participate. We developed simple study goals and built a list of questions that everyone could use. It wasn't overly processed or scientific. Our goal was to connect employees with the people they were solving problems for. Great things came out of this program.

A good example comes from QuickBooks, Intuit's small business financial management software and one of the leading small business applications with over 3 million users online alone. Before implementing the Follow Me Home program, we had always heard from home-based businesses (one of the large segments within the small business market) that "it's important to keep good financial records." We envisioned organized folders with bank statements, a receipt tracking system, tracking of monthly expense totals, and so on. We were so wrong!

After we implemented the Follow Me Home program, during a stint of observational sessions, we asked customers to show us their financial records and where and how they stored them. We found things like shoeboxes of receipts under the kitchen sink next to the cleaning supplies and dog brush. We found pretty boxes with stacks of bank statements, vendor statements, and invoices in random order. While customers believed they were organized, our vision of what "organized" meant was significantly different from theirs. Knowing this, we began to think differently about the application and how users input their data. It wasn't until we'd conducted several of these scrappy observational sessions that we could disprove our hypothesis that "good financial records" meant any sort of organized system. It wasn't until then that we could demonstrate to our company what "good financial records" actually meant to our users. This is only one example of many where the ongoing Follow Me Home program markedly influenced the direction of the QuickBooks product line.

Another great byproduct of ongoing connection with our customers was a broad appreciation of the pain our customers experienced and a strong motivation to fix it. As we talked about in the Groundwork Pillar II: Actionable Persona chapter, engineers who participated in these sessions would fix issues over a weekend after observing the pain they saw. It wasn't because it came up in the backlog or that they were assigned the task. It was because they saw the pain, first-hand, and empathized with it.

Participating in the Follow Me Home program eventually became part of most employees' compensation plans because it was so successful at infusing customer insights into our every-day decision making, resulting in customer delight and significant growth in each of the spaces where Intuit operated.

We're not saying that scrappy research has to become a company-wide effort to successfully drive delight and growth (though we recommend it). What we are saying is that ongoing simple connections to customers and prospects drive better product decisions and broader team commitment.

PRACTICE IN ACTION: OPENTABLE

There are multiple types of scrappy research, and in this chapter, we focused mostly on direct interviews. We also dabble a bit with observational sessions in the Individualized Needs chapter. We've found that interviews and observational sessions are the easiest and fastest way to connect and empathize with your customer. They're super easy to get up and running and you could have actionable learning in days. We also never lose the thrill of those aha! moments when we discover an unmet need through our discussion or observation, and actually see or hear it firsthand. It's the product manager's equivalent of finding an ancient treasure in an archaeological dig. There are, however, other great techniques you can use. We'll highlight a few that are simple and incredibly useful, albeit a little less scrappy than interviews.

Our friend and product super star Elizabeth Casey led product at OpenTable for over seven years during a time of incredible growth. She talked to us about how they went about unlocking the restaurant side of demand. OpenTable was growing and getting customers (diners) to adopt the app felt straightforward—after all, the only alternative at that time was calling the restaurant. Offering restaurant bookings online removed an obvious pain for diners. Despite OpenTable's rapid growth in user base, they found that restaurants underrepresented their availability to diners in the app. OpenTable needed to grow this number so there would be more availability when diners tried to book a table, but also to increase booking for their restaurants. This was an important problem to solve, and critical for business success.

Elizabeth and her team needed to increase their availability by 10%, which was a stretch at the time. Elizabeth told us they realized they had to move beyond the fast, obvious solutions. For example, one easy option was to just increase marketing—visit more restaurants and convince them to join the network, or incentivize sales to motivate restaurants to give OpenTable more seats. What they did instead was park themselves at various restaurants and observe (as Elizabeth says, "observe, observe, and observe more."). What they saw was a chaotic, dynamic environment, with the host/manager making rapid in-the-moment decisions. They observed what the hosts wrote down, what the hosts communicated to staff, and how they communicated it. Then the team did something brilliant in the name of scrappy research. They took over a restaurant one evening, and Elizabeth and her team became the staff. They got the pre-shift training, learned to set up tables, and took diners' orders. They lived the chaos and developed a deep empathy for how the restaurant operated in real time.

What they learned were several key root cause issues relevant to the fundamental design of their app, and how they had failed the needs of a busy staff. And because of those failures, the restaurant staff's workaround was to limit the number of tables made available to OpenTable. While this might seem a little less scrappy than interviews or observational in terms of research logistics, it was set up with only one restaurant over one shift. The team's ability to think creatively about how they could learn through first-hand experience made the research much more impactful. While they might have learned something by just observing, the empathy created by doing the work themselves changed the way they connected with the customer (restaurant staff) problem.

As a result of the insights gleaned from this single session with the restaurant, Elizabeth and team went back to their design and development teams with a very clear problem statement crafted based on their deep experience, observation, and insight. They were able to create a new, sophisticated, and simple feature that allowed the staff to respond in real time to diners' needs. One of OpenTable's customers said the app had the brain of their best manager. The change was seamless and invisible to diners. That, friends, is what the Groundwork is all about!

It's the combination of developing a hypothesis around the problem and persona, then doing the hands-on work—scrappy research—which leads to solutions that delight customers and drive growth.

SUMMARY

Let's recap.

- Scrappy research is a small number of structured customer interactions to test your most pressing hypotheses within 5 working days.
- Five to seven interviews are all you need as long as:
  - You talk to people who have the same profile as one another
  - You focus on a small number of critical hypotheses
  - Your questions are consistent and focused on extremes so you can identify themes
  - You're open to surprise
  - You probe deeply to get to the root cause

- Create a pipeline or repeatable method to identify research participants. Be creative. Once you have this, the ongoing practice of learning quickly becomes a reality.
- Make sure you close the loop by communicating not only what the team learned, but also what the business should do about it.

■ ■ ■

8

PRACTICE III:
GETTING COMMITMENT

A PRODUCT person's job is to be a thought-leader *and* to execute effectively. It's a unique challenge that only a few functional roles within a company experience. As product leaders, we must influence and gain commitment across multiple functions and leaders; and usually, none of them report directly to you. This unique aspect of our job is partly what makes being a product person so fun (and exhausting at times)! So, we would be remiss if we didn't discuss gaining commitment across complex organizations as one of the most critical practices a product leader should master. Whether you are a chief product officer or new product manager, proficiency in this practice dictates your success.

Getting commitment is required as the first step when implementing any strategy or product decision, big or small. Without commitment, agreement is moot. Commitment is something that many people in business, and in life, don't understand and are caught off guard when they realize they never had it.

We define Commitment as:

A state in which the decision-maker(s) and critical stakeholders intend to and follow through on making the accommodations necessary to implement a decision, while holding themselves accountable for their part in the success of the project, regardless of whether they agree with the decision.

Let's break this down.

What do we mean by critical stakeholders? These are the business people who will be significantly impacted by the decision; not customers—you've already done the Groundwork to propose a product decision that meets your customer's needs. Stakeholders are people like operational partners (internal and external), your development team, your manufacturing partners, your support team, and so on. These are the folks that have to take action in order to ensure success of the project.

What do we mean by the necessary accommodations? This could be anything required to execute, such as funding, human resources, operational or technical tradeoffs.

The last part of our definition of commitment is important. We want to get to a situation where people may not agree with the decision, but they are committed to it because they understand how the decision was made and why. In this section, we talk about the elements involved in giving you the best chance of getting commitment on decisions: collecting the data required, presenting your case, and pressure testing commitment.

WHAT COMMITMENT IS NOT

Getting commitment is very different from getting a head nod in the meeting where you propose a product decision. Many times, the head nod of agreement is taken as a "go." But we all know that a lot happens after people walk out of a meeting. People are bombarded by inputs from others, conflicting priorities, and shiny objects that potentially change a head nod to an eventual head shake.

Getting Commitment Doesn't Mean Consensus

If you strive for consensus, you could be waiting a long time. Some cultures require consensus. And to those of you working in those cultures, our hat's off to you. We respect anyone that perseveres through consensus-building even at the cost of progress. There is a better way.

Instead of consensus, strive for a shared vision (we touched on this earlier in the book) of the data and in light of the decision, get a commitment to the actions required to be successful. Shared vision sounds like corporate jargon, we realize. But as you already know, it's a concept that has stuck with us in our careers, because of how powerful it is. We strive for everyone impacted by a decision to understand how we got to a decision, versus just telling them what the decision is. We do this by communicating compellingly clear logic, data, and customer insight, all of which we obtain through the Groundwork and Practices we've explained up to this point.

The next time you see a lot of head nods in a meeting, do a double take and make sure you actually have a shared vision and a commitment on the actions that will result from the decision.

WHY GETTING COMMITMENT IS IMPORTANT

If you don't have commitment, multiple rehashing of the decisions occur, actions are delayed or never taken, and decisions are overturned. When was the last time you thought one of the decisions made was a done deal, only to hear through the grapevine that your [enter organizational function here] manager said, "I just don't think that's going to work." Or "I talked to Joe and he said that we really should be doing this instead." Or "Can we get back together to talk about this? My team is just not on board and doesn't understand why we're doing this." *Are we hitting a nerve yet?*

The reasons for getting commitment are obvious. If your leaders or stakeholders aren't committed to executing or stomaching the risks of the decision, or addressing challenges that come up along the way, then a head nod on a decision is merely lip service.

SUCCESSFULLY GETTING COMMITMENT

There are many books on leadership, decision making, and influence. We are students of many of them. We aren't going to repeat their teachings here. We will, however, point out some factors that ensure you, as a leader in product management, gain commitment, taking into account the unique aspects of the organizational function you are in.

Clarify Roles and Responsibilities in a Given Decision: RACI

RACI isn't new. But it's one of the most important ways we know to ensure clarity in the decision-making process and avoid decision delays. RACI is a decision framework that clarifies who the decision-makers are, who the critical stakeholders are (those who are on the hook to give or do something to execute on the decision you are proposing), and who just needs to be informed.

If you already know this framework, then you can skip this section. For those of you that don't, get excited. Making your organization adopt this very simple framework will wipe out one big challenge to achieving efficient and effective decision making across complex cross-functional organizations. The RACI acronym defines each role as follows:

- **R →** **Responsible.** Who is the person responsible for driving the decision to closure and getting the data and inputs needed to make the right decision? This is usually one person, or two people max.
- **A →** **Approver.** Who makes the final decision? This should never be more than two people. We see the most difficulties getting commitment where three to five different people think they are decision-makers, which leaves the Responsible person frustrated as the decision vacillates.
- **C →** **Consulted.** Who has critical input for the decision? These are people who either have data, experience, or knowledge that informs the decision, or are critically impacted by the decision (e.g., cost, resources, required tradeoffs). Don't confuse Consulted with Approvers. Many times, when there is confusion about who makes a decision, it's because a Consulted person assumes they

are an Approver. There is no set number of Consulted individuals.

Let's say you are the 'R' in a decision. You might need to ask around at the organization about who should be consulted. Especially if you're newer to your role or the company, or if the decision involves a product space that you're less familiar with. Your goal is to ensure the best decision for the business, so seeking the critical inputs is your job as the Responsible party.

| → **Informed.** Who needs to know that a decision is made and what that decision is? This could be a whole host of people, from teams to divisions, to the entire company.

Make sure you spend time upfront documenting and getting a shared vision on these roles with the team before going too far into the analysis and proposal phases of decision making. Remember to constantly reiterate these roles in most communications and meetings leading up to the final decision. This ensures that everyone remembers what role they play, and avoids surprise if a decision is made without their "approval."

We can't tell you how many times decisions are delayed or overturned because it wasn't clear who made the decisions or who should have been consulted when formulating the decision. That's why we use this tried and true RACI decision model. First introduced in the 1950s, RACI was originally called the "Decision Rights Matrix." There are variations, like RASCI, ARCI, and DACI, but all are meant to ensure clarity of roles and responsibilities for any given project or decision. It's used by a variety of companies, from the likes of eBay, Amazon, and Procter & Gamble, to the U.S. Department of Defense.

Again, the product leader role is a unique position. It requires influencing and leading many functional teams across the organization without direct-reporting relationships. Some people you need to gain commitment from may be higher up in the organization than you. So, specifying who is making a decision and who will be consulted are critical to successfully getting closure on decisions.

Demonstrate Customer and Data-Backed Decisions

If you didn't expect this after everything you've read so far, then we suggest going back and reading the Groundwork Pillars and the other

Practice chapters again. Decisions are best made outside the opinion zone. Here's how Peter Karpas, former VP and GM of North America Small & Medium Business at PayPal framed this:

HPO (highest paid opinion)   *beats O (opinion)*
RESEARCH   *beats HPO*
DATA   *beats RESEARCH*

....and product managers (and many product leaders) are NEVER the HPO.

So, set yourself up for success. What data (customer, market, operational, etc.) do you need to make the decision and get the required commitment? We like to make a list of questions that need to be answered as inputs to any given decision and then list the data available that could answer those questions. If we won't be able to get targeted data (because of time or other restrictions), we try to identify proxies or hypotheses that might help make better-informed gut decisions. Of course, we'll need to conduct scrappy research to prove or disprove those hypotheses in short order. Here are some tips on how to present compelling data and customer-backed decisions.

- Make sure you let the customer speak by using actual quotes, pictures, video, or audio from the sessions, when possible.
- Summarize the most relevant data and corresponding "why this is important" points. Don't show a laundry list of irrelevant data that forces your audience to do their own sifting.
- List any big gaps, where there's no data and present any hypotheses that drove a decision and show when and how you're going to verify them. This will inspire confidence among your stakeholders that you are or will be using data to drive the decision and will pivot if necessary.
- List the givens that impact your decision. For example: "Decision outcome depends on platform refactoring completion, expected by the end of the year." Givens allow the team to be aware of both timing and risks that are potentially outside the control of

the team executing on the decision. Listing the givens helps avoid unnecessary debate, questions, and potential surprises.

The point here is to get targeted data that not only drives the decision, but also tackles potential objections. Keep your conversations with Consulted and Approver groups as data based versus opinion based. And where you need to make some hypotheses (which is fine), point them out and have a plan to prove or disprove them. Hypotheses are not unusual, as long as they are justifiable. As long as they make intuitive sense, teams are usually okay with moving forward as long as they know you will get data and verify them and or change course before it's too late.

Democratize the Data

Many product leaders fail at this tip. We frequently see decisions made by a product manager who cherry picks the data they believe supports the decision they're proposing and shares only that very specific data with stakeholders. Regardless of whether the decision is right and how true your intentions are, cherry-picking breeds skepticism and a lack of trust from those who may have other data that leads them to favor a different decision. The whole discussion gets derailed and your reputation as a customer advocate and unbiased business leader begins to tarnish.

Make sure everyone has the same information. Even if you need to spend a bit of extra time in a meeting bringing people up to speed on the key learning and data points to build clear logic for your decision and the options you decided not to go with, do it! Make sure it's a summary of all the data you've discovered, obtained through conversations with your Consulted group, and coalesced into a logic that the team can understand. Build a story that makes sense instead of showing one or two data points that paint half a picture. You may not get to consensus, but if everyone in the room understands the data that brought you to a decision, and no one has additional data to counter it, it's hard not to commit.

We spoke about 99designs a couple times in this book. They are a great example of how a company can democratize data by requiring everyone to maintain a connection with customers on a regular basis. Ashish, the former chief product office for 99designs, expected *everyone*, not just the product team, to maintain some connection with users daily. Employees would engage in the many channels where customers provided feedback and asked questions. The company attributes much of their ability to make durable decisions and drive customer delight to the ongoing practice of this scrappy customer research.

So instead of a product person presenting customer feedback to their functional stakeholders, each and every employee hears (and feels) the same pain and delight directly from the customer. We are fond of this double whammy. Not only is the data democratized because everyone hears directly from customers, but all product decisions are based on customer insight versus opinion. High-five, 99designs!

Demonstrate Empathy for Your Stakeholders

"People listen better if they feel that you have understood them. They tend to think that those who understand them are intelligent and sympathetic people whose own opinions may be worth listening to. If you want the other side to appreciate your interests, begin by demonstrating that you appreciate theirs." This is a quote from Roger Fisher's book *Getting to Yes: Negotiating Agreement Without Giving In, 3rd Edition* (Penguin, 2011). We love this book (and this quote) and recommend you read it. It's by two Harvard pros who broke the code on negotiating. But we particularly like this quote because as a product leader, you need to not only gather ideas from different perspectives but you also need to show that you care and understand the impact a decision has on different stakeholders.

As product leaders our decisions impact so many different organizational functions in the organization. To gain commitment, it's critical to master the skills of listening, understanding, and demonstrating empathy for any stakeholders impacted by a decision.

What does this mean operationally? It means you meet with your functional counterparts to understand the implications of the different options you are considering when making a decision. It means you ask for feedback when you formulate your proposed decision. We are keen on floating trial balloons for proposed decisions to the stakeholders who might resist the decision. This lets us hear their feedback and they feel heard and part of the final decision.

Ask yourself the following key questions before deciding, or at least before presenting a decision, especially when you're looking for big commitments from the audience you are presenting to:

- Do you know the impact the options you're considering has on stakeholders ("know" being the operative word; not guessing)?
- What do stakeholders need to be successful if the decision is approved?
- Do stakeholders feel like they've been consulted in this process?
- How do you communicate what you've learned from stakeholders in your decision proposal, such that they feel heard and understood?

Address Anticipated Naysayers

Let's face it, we all have naysayers in our organizations. Naysayers are strong influencers who object no matter what, think they have a better idea, or believe an alternative option is the right path. And sometimes that alternative path won't be one of the primary options already being considered and analyzed. It happens. And some of these influential naysayers can derail the decision process. These folks have to be addressed to get broad commitment.

But there's hope. We use the following list of good practices:

1. **Identify any highly influential naysayers who could derail the decision-making process.** They may or may not be a primary Consulted, but they hold strong influence in the company. We've seen tenured engineers, senior leaders of non-impacted organizational functions, board members, and investors be naysayers. They could have the ear of the CEO, your executive leader, or your CTO.
2. **Understand their point of view.** A simple feedback gathering session might be in order. Trial ballooning a proposed decision is a good way of getting their point of view. Understand what their objection or their desired path is and why.
3. **Use data.** When possible, to do a quick thought exercise on what the path they suggest looks like, asking these questions:

- How does their idea or path measure up to the criteria you are using to decide? Evaluate it with any data you have available.
- What are the critical dependencies (e.g., technical, manufacturing, political, resourcing) in executing their idea or path?
- What would you have to prioritize in the product (e.g., features, infrastructure, roadmap items) to make their path successful and how does that differ from the proposed decision path?
- Are there other, possibly unforeseen, operational requirements for their path (e.g., marketing, support, operations)?

These are questions you should already be asking of the obvious options in your decision, but they are important to ask as they relate to the strong naysayer's path as well. Don't make this a huge, time-consuming expedition. We don't usually spend more than a 30-minute discussion and a 30-minute thought exercise fleshing through their desired path to understand the implications it has, building a case as to why it isn't the right thing to do considering the criteria at hand. Or maybe it is? There have been times when their perspectives bring new thinking to the table that must be considered.

Always anticipate who your most influential naysayers will be and gather the information you need to understand their perspective. Do quick due diligence to understand what it would take to execute their presumed path so that you can confidently speak to it. It not only ensures you haven't missed anything, but it also shows the naysayer that you are thinking broadly and considering all options, not just what you are proposing, makes them feel heard, and sets you up for a much higher probability of commitment.

PRACTICE IN ACTION: LYCOS

Our friend Jana Eggers was always a superstar at getting commitment. We always saw her as someone who pushed through organizational complexity to get big things done in whatever role she was in. Jana has led product for decades at companies like Blackbaud, Intuit, and Lycos. Today she's the CEO of Nara Logics, Inc., a wildly successful startup with a patented synaptic intelligence platform that helps companies build business advisors from their data.

We're going to take you through a flashback, when Jana was a product leader at Lycos. For old-school tech folks, you know what Lycos is. For the young babes in the woods, Lycos was one of the original internet search engines back in the mid-1990s. The best description of Lycos back then is a cross between Google and Yahoo; a search engine and content portal combo.

Jana's team led search. In those early days, search engines focused on searching only websites and Jana's team was on the leading edge, developing technology to search additional content sources; namely FTP servers. The FTP search project involved highly complex technology, making it difficult to explain to partners, advertisers, and users alike. So, if Lycos wanted to sell it to the masses, the project would entail heavy lifting from not only the product development team, but also the operational and marketing teams.

Jana needed marketing to figure out how to make users understand the value of expanded search functionality. She needed the ad sales team to explain the benefit expanded search would have on less tech-savvy advertisers and learn how to sell it. And she needed operations to capture and report on new sources of content. There were a host of challenges to overcome to make the search expansion successful and it would take time and resources away from the pre-existing larger, more easily understood mainstay operations for content, ad sales, and website search.

Jana worked with all the company stakeholders to understand what it would take to bring this innovation to market and got the head nod from everyone. The entire company knew how ground-breaking this search tech was for the company. Lycos was the known leader of search at the time. Conceptually, it was a no brainer and each team was proud and excited to be a part of the project. Yet they failed to get traction; Jana watched as other projects were prioritized, leaving her search team behind. She didn't know why. That is, until she was invited to present to the C-level team, which is when she began to understand.

After presenting on a different project, she was invited to stay and listen in on the rest of the executive staff discussion. In doing so, she experienced an "aha!" moment. She realized that all teams were literally competing against each other to progress the fastest in order to win resources. And it was the projects that were easiest to make progress on that got the most attention and garnered the most resource allocation. Thus, teams prioritized whatever would ensure resources and recognition from the CEO. To Jana, it was almost like watching a sales meeting with teams (and projects) competing against one another.

This, in and of itself, isn't necessarily a bad thing. Every CEO and leadership team cultivates their own culture and habits that work for them. For Lycos, this seemed to work. After all, they were a hugely successful tech company. But it taught Jana a good lesson about getting commitment that she carries with her everywhere she goes. The lesson Jana learned was that she needed to understand the priorities of her critical stakeholders. She began by asking stakeholders these questions:

- Where does this project fall on your priority list?
- What else are you working on? What is more important, and why?
- When might you be able to start this project?
- How long do you think it will take?
- What else do you need in order to get started?
- How can I help?

As she hit roadblocks, she focused on "being polite, but not bashful." When stakeholders told her that their priorities precluded the team from taking on her project in the timeframe she expected, she would ask questions like:

- Sounds like you're in a tough spot, can I talk to [insert boss' name here]?
- Are you okay with me chatting with [inserts boss' name here] to see if I can relieve pressure on your other priorities to move this one up?

In some ways, product leaders are lucky. They have a unique opportunity to engage with and know the leaders of almost every function in a company. We get to know their traits, like who's a pain in the butt, who's an analytical thinker, who's driven by ego, and so on. That gives us a leg up when negotiating with these folks.

Jana's never been afraid to ask tough questions in a group setting. When going around the room and asking how each team prioritizes the project and everyone puts the project at a priority 2, except one person who puts it at a priority 10, there's some value in hearing the broader team prioritization levels. It creates perspective across the organization, and peer pressure doesn't hurt either, but we digress.

There will be people who are less willing to play ball. And no, you don't strong arm them in a group setting. You pull people aside and listen to discover the root cause behind their lack of commitment. Remember the 5-Whys technique we talked about? It's very valuable here.

So, what happened with Jana's project? The FTP search project got finished of course, and Lycos went on to make history in search, and got acquired by Terra Networks for over $12 billion. Lycos is still in business today. Jana has continued to use those early lessons in alignment and commitment throughout her career. She not only makes sure to look for the "yes" during the meeting, but she also spends the time probing to understand the context and priorities of each stakeholder and works to resolve any potential hurdles to get projects prioritized.

SUMMARY

We've added a few practices to your product leadership skills arsenal that drive a higher probability of getting commitment across your critical stakeholders. As you practice getting commitment, make sure you:

- Define and communicate with everyone who will drive the closure of the decision (the Responsible), make the decision (the Approver), and who will be a subject matter expert (the Consulted) in the process.

- Infuse data and customer insights into your decision logic to avoid opinion-based discussion.
- Give everyone the same data.
- Anticipate the naysayers and their objections, and address them head-on.
- Listen and learn from your stakeholders and infuse what you learn into your decisions.

■ ■ ■

CLOSING THOUGHTS

WE'RE SO passionate about the impact that the Groundwork can have for you and your teams and for your products and your customers. We unequivocally believe the path to making great products starts with defining the problem to be solved, getting a clear understanding of the customer, then connecting with customers directly. As we close the book and come to the end of this journey together, we want to provide an easy way of getting started on bringing these pillars and practices into your organization. After all, we're all about doing the work. Here's a way to get started:

GROUNDWORK PILLAR 1: CONVERGENT PROBLEM STATEMENT

Let's ensure your team is all solving exactly the same problem. Take our Convergent Problem Statement template on page 24 to your next product meeting and have everyone complete it individually; this will take all of 5 minutes. Gather all the templates, and see what picture it forms. Are your teams all on the same page? Share the different statements with your team and have them work together to create one single problem statement they all agree on.

GROUNDWORK PILLAR 2: ACTIONABLE PERSONA

Let's get your team to have a usable, workable persona. Ask everyone on your team to take 5-10 minutes and fill out the Persona Template on page 48, then bring these to your next team meeting. Compare them— are they consistent? Do the customer statements come from research, or are they completely imagined? Where are the big gaps in customer understanding? Have a volunteer bring these different versions together to a single persona your team can use.

GROUNDWORK PILLAR 3: INDIVIDUALIZED NEEDS

Let's make sure your team is clear on customer needs. Once you have the problem-persona combination, then ask each member of your team to assign a weight using our set of criteria (level of pain, pervasiveness, cost and strategic impact) that we share on pages 88-89. This is a great exercise for a team discussion. Are there differences in how the different criteria are rated? Work together to get a shared understanding of what's important.

Going beyond our Pillars, our three Practices—Developing the Hypotheses, Conducting Scrappy Research, and Getting Commitment— represent the skills we want everyone on the team to have. In our ideal world, we see you all practice each of these weekly—sharing hypothesis in team meetings and getting feedback, making sure that a customer research readout is part of every sprint planning meeting, adding a picture or video or quote from a customer in every presentation that a product manager makes. We'll keep quietly fantasizing that you're doing just that.

As you introduce the Groundwork and practices into your organization, remember it takes time to change culture, mindset and behaviors. Start with modeling the behavior: show what customer data was important in making key business decisions, describe the hypotheses you have and why you believe them to be true, expose the tradeoffs you're making and the thought process behind the choice—people are listening. Consider putting the application of the Groundwork and practices into an individual's objectives and goals. Review the Groundwork in every key product meeting, and hold your team accountable to consistently produce the set of deliverables associated with the Groundwork. With this ongoing attention you will find that teams will steadily *get better at making better products.*

■ ■ ■

ACKNOWLEDGMENTS

WRITING THIS book was both more fun, and at the same time much harder than we ever expected. We have so many exceptional former colleagues, an incredible network of friends, a valuable team, and a supportive family to thank. We'd like to start with the generous people who are featured in this book and have directly assisted us in this writing journey by spending time talking to us and sharing their stories. They've inspired us and helped us become better product leaders and we are deeply grateful to all these wonderful people: Jessica Barker who has one of the most clear and focused ways of honing in on the right problem to solve we've seen; Elizabeth Casey whose creativity in research taught us new ways to think; Ashish Desai who has an unrelenting passion for solving for the customer; Jana Eggers, whose leadership style showed us how to galvanize an organization; Peter Karpas, whose energy and passion for customers is infectious; Ginny Lee, who has a superpower that turns simple customer insights into winning pivots in a business;

Joanne Norton whose patience in getting to the right customer insight is simply inspiring; Andrew Tokeley who embodies a passion for learning from customers that touches everyone around him; and Brent Tworetzky whose sharp intellect constantly uncovers the right questions to ask at the right time. We hope the interviews we present in this book from each of them successfully capture a small part of their incredible creativity, leadership and customer focus.

We have been fortunate to work with some exceptional companies in our career as we learned and practiced the craft of product management. It is, however, in our coaching practice that we have had the opportunity to put into practice the best of what we had learned. Thank you to all the clients who trusted us with the growth and development of their product teams. We are grateful to every one of you.

We're novices in the book publishing world. We literally couldn't have launched this book without our amazing team; David Miles, our designer who patiently gave us version after version of the cover, and helped us land on an image we love. Jill Weisberg, our editor who made us rewrite way more than we ever expected, we thought we wrote reasonably well before we met her. We're grateful for every sentence she touched. Vanessa Campos has been a miracle worker, she's taken the complexity of the publishing world, and broken it down step by step, and given us a plan we can follow. We are so grateful for her patience, answering endless questions and guiding us thoughtfully and enthusiastically through the entire publication and launch process. We also want to send a special thank-you to Todd Sattersten who led us to Vanessa, and helped us navigate the world of publishing. His kind and generous coaching helped us make the right choices for how we would get this book out into the world.

We've leaned on many colleagues and friends to pre-read the book, and give us feedback. Our heartfelt thanks to each of you who took the time to read the excerpts, and for your warm and generous support. We learn from each of you every day. We are also blessed with a network of friends who have patiently listened to this book's progress, given us thoughtful feedback, and encouraged us when we needed it. We are beyond grateful to them all. Finally, a brief personal word from each of us.

From Vidya:

Thank you to my family: my beautiful children, Jasmine, Alisha & Sam who happily cheer on every milestone like I just won a race. I'm so lucky to be your mom. My brother, Giri, who I can always count on for tough, and always loving, advice. Thank you for your steadfast support. Thank you to my parents for their love and support throughout my life, you gave us a foundation that made so many adventures possible.

Thank you to my special circle of friends that keep me laughing, and know exactly what to say to keep me going when I need an encouraging word. A heartfelt thank you to Dave Torrence and Alex Sun for their generous gift of time to start writing this book when I was still a corporate executive. To the many product, development, design, marketing and business leaders that I'm so fortunate to call my friends, you know who you are, I admire and adore you. One of the very first product leaders I admired was Heather, and now we get to work together every day. I can't think of a better person to go on this wild ride with.

Thank you to all the teams I've been privileged to lead. I've taken every single thing you've taught me and put it into my coaching. I hope I do you proud.

And to my husband, Chris, who is my steady rock—thank you for always believing in me.

From Heather:

Thanks pop and mom for giving me the drive and confidence in life to be who I am today. I know that I can achieve whatever I set my mind to, including writing this book, because of your support and the engrained "throw some dirt on it" attitude! And to Sissy; you are my role model; in personal drive, in faith, and gratitude for life…and for getting me off my ass and kicking me into gear whenever the chips are down.

Thanks to my lovely friends who always inspire me to do and be better. Without your support, honest feedback, and inspiration by example, this book wouldn't have happened; including my partner in crime on this fantastic journey, Vidya.

To all of the wonderful product leaders that have taught me so much. Special thanks to Peter Karpas, my friend, who always inspires me with his passion for great customer experiences (and music!). To Laurel

Lee and Craig Carlson who first taught me what sitting in the shoes of my customer really felt like. To Intuit; the company and leadership from whom I've learned so much from. It was there that I learned the discipline of focusing on the customer problem over anything else is the foundation to building a winning business.

And to the love of my life. Lee, you have been there through the challenges over this journey and have given my heart a place to rest at the end of every crazy day. Thank you for your love and continued faith in me.

■ ■ ■

ABOUT THE AUTHORS

VIDYA DINAMANI is the co-founder for Product Rebels where she exercises her passion for coaching product leaders and teams. She has over 18 years of experience specializing in business and technology strategy development and product design, development and management.

Vidya has held multiple executive roles at leading companies, including executive positions leading Innovation and Design, Product Management and Marketing at Mitchell International, as well as Director of Customer Experience for TurboTax. She also served as Director of Business Operations for Intuit where she was first met Heather. Vidya loves working with early stage companies, helping them establish their Groundwork, and serves as advisor to multiple companies. A holder of 9 U.S. patents for software technology, Vidya earned a B.S. in Physics from Victoria University in Wellington, New Zealand, and a Masters from Carnegie Mellon University in Pittsburgh, Pennsylvania. She is also a certified Net Promoter Associate.

HEATHER SAMARIN is the co-founder of Product Rebels and has over 17 years of experience in delighting customers through the design, development, and management of customer experiences within both B2B and B2C marketing and product management.

Heather started her career and spent over 13 years at Intuit where she met Vidya and built her passion for customer-driven decision making. It was in her positions as Director of QuickBooks Enterprise and VP of Product Management in the TurboTax business where her love for new product design and innovation began. She and her team launched Intuit's QuickBooks Enterprise business, an up-market QuickBooks product that is now achieving over $50MM in revenue. Since then, she has held C-level and senior roles within multiple industries like social gaming and healthcare markets where she led product strategy and new product design and development. She holds a B.S. in Finance from California State University and an MBA in Marketing from Santa Clara University.

■ ■ ■

RESOURCES FOR PRODUCT LEADERS

If you like what you've read and would like to bring these concepts into your team with our help, we're here to help in a variety of ways:

Signature Groundwork Team Program

Transform your product team in just six weeks. Our private, blended learning program for product management teams establishes a common taxonomy and approach to developing great experiences.

In less than three hours a week, your team will learn the Groundwork Pillars and Practices and apply them to the products they work on day-to-day.

Our blended learning approach makes it easy for every PM to learn individually; our direct application to your product means that you'll see meaningful impact immediately and the learned concepts will be retained. The weekly coaching from a tenured product executive ensures a faster time to value to the business. Product Rebels works in partnership with you as the product management leader in driving a transformation of thinking and practice across the team.

Signature Public Workshop

Send one of your product managers to participate in our signature public workshop. Held over 5 days in five, 90-minute sessions makes the training easy to integrate into a work week.

Designed for product managers wanting to learn and apply the Groundwork framework and tools to their product, while learning from their peers, and getting real time feedback and coaching from a tenured product management executive. We cover the 3 Pillars and 3 Practices of the Groundwork framework while openly discussing and applying the tools and templates to their product during the workshop.

Custom Training Programs

We can work with you to create a workshop based on your company's needs. Whether that's working on role clarity, improving agile practices to include the right product deliverables, or ways to think about new product development that are customer-driven. We have lots of fun partnering with companies to bring them the right training leveraging all the Groundwork Pillars and Practices.

Keynote Speaking

We love speaking, and have given talks all over the world (ask us about Lviv). We especially enjoy talking to organizations about the value and benefits of customer-driven product management. We have given 1-hour talks to leadership teams (where product management is poorly understood), to development teams (when there is a recognized need to shift to more product/customer vs engineering), and organizations (for an inspiring talk on the value of listening to customers).

To learn more about these workshops visit us at **ProductGroundwork.com**

To learn more about Product Rebels and our other offerings visit us at **ProductRebels.com**

Interested in bringing Product Rebels to your organization? Email us at **info@productrebels.com**

BONUS MATERIAL

Be sure to get your online bonus material at **ProductGroundwork.com/ resources.** You'll receive access to supplemental material designed to enhance your reading experience, help you bring the Groundwork to your team with free downloads, templates, and stay up to date with all things product.

INDEX